THE SPECTRUM OF THE SACRED

RANCHI ANTHROPOLOGY SERIES-6

RANCHI ANTHROPOLOGY SERIES

1. Process, Performance, and Pilgrimage: A Study in Comparative Symbology/ Victor Witter Turner
2. Development of Researches in Anthropology in India: Bihar-A Case Study/ L.P. Vidyarthi and V.S. Upadhyay
3. Nature Man Spirit Complex in Tribal India/ R.S. Mann and Vijay S. Sahay
4. Microevolution/ B.M. Das
5. Tribal Festivals of Bihar: A Functional Analysis/ Ajit K. Singh

---

About the Author

Bidyanath Saraswati (*b.* 1932) is Research Professor in Indira Gandhi National Centre for the Arts, New Delhi; former Professor of Anthropology in North Eastern Hill University, Shillong. Professor Saraswati's major publications include: Contributions to the understanding of Indian civilization; Pottery making cultures and Indian classical cultural tradition; Brahmanic ritual traditions; The spectrum of the Sacred; and Ascetics of Kashi: an Anthropological exploration (with Surajit Sinha.

RANCHI ANTHROPOLOGY SERIES-6

Gen. Editor: **L.P. VIDYARTHI**

THE SPECTRUM OF THE SACRED

Essays on the Religious Traditions of India

BAIDYANATH SARASWATI

CONCEPT PUBLISHING COMPANY PVT. LTD.

NEW DELHI-110059

ISBN-13: 978-81-7022-132-6

Edition 2017

Published and Printed by

Concept
Since 1974

Concept Publishing Company Pvt. Ltd.
A/15-16, Commercial Block, Mohan Garden
New Delhi-110059 (India)
T: 25351460, 25351794, *F*: 091-11-25357109
E: publishing@conceptpub.com, W: www.conceptpub.com
Editorial Office: H-13, Bali Nagar, New Delhi-110 015, India.

To
the sacred memory of

Daijee
(DURGAWATI DEVI)

who mothered me
most affectionately

GENERAL EDITOR'S INTRODUCTION

THE Department of Anthropology of Ranchi University celebrated its Silver Jubilee in 1978. Again, it received the recognition of being the only U.G.C. Centre of Special Assistance in Anthropology in the country almost in the same year. During the tenure of my Presidentship of the International Union of Anthropological and Ethnological Sciences (1973-78) as well as Xth ICAES (1978), the Department was also called upon to perform several academic and professional roles involving it at the international level.

With this background, we ventured to launch a new series of publications entitled "Ranchi Anthropology Series" in the year 1980. This series is designed to provide a short but scholarly treatment of key problem-areas in anthropology. Under this series, in addition to lectures delivered at Ranchi by visiting scholars of national and international repute, we have also been publishing the theoretically oriented research work of local scholars as well as proceedings of national and international level seminars and symposia. The present volume, the VIth in the series, is by Dr. Baidyanath Saraswati who was visiting professor in the Department of Special Assistance in Anthropology at Ranchi University in 1979-80. As his assignment, Dr. Saraswati gave a series of lectures and systematised his own thinking and writing on the issues of the sacred complex.

Since the publication of my book, *The Sacred Complex in Hindu Gaya* (1961), some of my students have earnestly followed the study of sacred complex, which has now acquired a place of significance in the anthropology of religion in general and Indian anthropology in particular. Baidyanath

Saraswati is one of those of my pupils who has consistently developed this theme and added up to the existing method of understanding sacred traditions. This volume is a collection of his ten essays reflecting what he calls the Indian vision of the sacred. Most of these essays have originated during his association with the Department of Anthropology, and at least two of them, published here for the first time, were delivered as Visiting Professorship lectures in anthropology at the Ranchi University. It was therefore appropriate enough to publish this volume under the Ranchi Anthropology Series.

All the ten essays, bearing cumulatively on a theory or concrete data, are the product of Saraswati's intellectual process. It would seem obvious that his thinking has developed over the years. The five essays grouped together as appendix, in part two, and written during the first decade of his work, constitute the primary material on the sacred complex; the first part, written later, illustrates the steps by which he has conceptualized the ethnographic data into a theory of the sacred complex. His work sets forth wider significance of my original and initial research, as he demonstrates unity in the diversities of sacred traditions in India, classifies cultures in relation to the modes of transmission of knowledge, and develops a theory which implies a continuum between the sacred and the secular. His interpretation of poetry and pilgrimage shows the widening areas of the sacred complex studies, as to how an orientation into the knowledge of the sacred complex can help generalization and understanding of language and ritual. Saraswati lends himself to certain provocative assumptions regarding the cosmological functions of ritual, which he has discussed only briefly in this book but hopes to work out at length in a later work towards a theory which he calls "transanthropology". While we look forward to his new theoretical considerations, the present volume is immensely satisfying.

I am happy to say that Baidyanath Saraswati's researches in the field of sacred complex have further sharpened the tools and have brought sophistication in analysis. The new supplementary effects have been added to my original work. Once the foundation stone is laid and the configuration is carried out, the preparation for the edifice is needed.

Director, U.G.C. Centre of Special Assistance in Anthropology and University Professor and Head, Department of Anthropology Ranchi University, Ranchi.

L.P. VIDYARTHI

6 March 1984

PREFACE

THE following ten essays, though not systematically connected, are strongly related in as much as they all reflect the Indian vision of the sacred. These are somewhat artificially stitched together in two parts. The first five essays, placed in Part One, are of a theoretical nature, covering the broad spectrum of the sacred. The first essay, "The concept of the sacred", highlights the basic difference between the Western notion of binary opposition and the Indian vision of non-dualism. It ventures to develop a theory which implies a continuum between the sacred and the secular. The second, "The sacred complex in Indian cultural traditions", examines the cultural foundations of the sacred and demonstrates how these different notions of the sacred, developed in three different cultural traditions, form a real set of religious phenomena. This point of unity in the cultural diversities of beliefs and behaviour is further developed and substantiated in the third essay, "The sacred journey: traditions of pilgrimage in India". The fourth essay, "The sacred: the proper context of poetry", points out that the sacred is the proper context of both primitive and classical poetry. Obviously, this comprehension of a totally sacralized human existence leaves no room for the sacred-profane or sacred-secular opposition. The fifth essay, "Understanding sacred traditions: an essay on the structure and functions of religion", is both a conclusion and a beginning. It is a conclusion, because the generalizations regarding the structure and functions of religion, made in this essay, are deeply related to the domain of the sacred—the subject matter of this book. This is also a beginning, because it defines the structure and functions of religion. Perhaps I should state—it is a bridge between the foregoing and the following. Part Two of this book provides supportive material, mostly descriptive in nature. In all these essays I draw heavily upon my own experience in the pursuit of studying the sacred traditions in India.

These essays, which were written on different occasions over a period of two decades, have been put together in one volume with a view to highlighting the integrability of the whole range of my ideas on the sacred. However, my search for a new perspective in religious research, which I call the transanthropological perspective, is continuing and this may eventually question the validity of some of my own ideas and interpretations as this little book offers. But unless such a perspective is clearly developed and brought into use the assumptions made in the following pages stand valid and relevant.

The first essay has been drawn upon a lecture which I delivered in 1979 at the Ranchi University Department of Anthropology; the fifth essay was also written there. The third, written in 1976, was my contribution to the Professor L.P. Vidyarthi Felicitation Volume, which, for some unfortunate reasons, has not yet appeared. The seventh essay was also written the same year for a proposed journal, which also has not yet seen the light of publication. The remaining essays were originally published as follows. The second essay was published in 1972, in Binod Chand Agrawal (ed.) *Anthropological Approaches to the Study of a Complex Society*; the fourth appeared in 1978, in *Man in India* 58(3); the sixth essay in 1974, in the *Journal of Social Research* 17(1); the eighth in 1965, in the *Journal of Social Research* 8(2); the ninth in 1963, in *Man in India* 43(2); the tenth in 1967, in *Man in India* 47(4). Most gratefully, I reproduce them here with only nominal changes.

This volume owes to the inspiration of my mentor, Professor L.P. Vidyarthi, whose monumental work on *The Sacred Complex in Hindu Gaya* marks the beginning of an anthropological tradition of studying the sacred places in India. Since the publication of this book in 1961, several scholars, mostly Professor Vidyarthi's students, have reported on a fairly large number of sacred places. But, unfortunately, most of them have ended up in a pale imitation, using the terms "sacred complex", "sacred geography", "sacred performances", and "sacred specialists" indiscriminately and substitutively for religion, shrines, rituals, and priests respectively. The Hindu

Gaya model of the sacred complex has been applied also to tribal religion. Surprisingly, none of these works has cared to define or discuss the Indian concept of the sacred, or to distinguish with certainty the sacred of the complex society from the sacred of the simpler society. I believe, in studies as this, one cannot possibly avoid posing the metaphysical issues. At any rate, the concept of the sacred complex, with all its forcefulness, deserves a more extended treatment than what it has so far received. Like so many others, my entry into the study of religion also owes to Professor Vidyarthi. My indebtedness to him is too great and too personal to be formally acknowledged. He has not only initiated me but has also supported me in countless ways to pursue this field of research and to carry on his tradition. Yet, in truth, notwithstanding his profound personal influence, I have somewhat drifted in my approach to the study of sacred traditions. However, if the ideas treated in this volume make any sense and impact, I will consider the deviation a happy extension of Professor Vidyarthi's work.

This volume was planned and partly written in 1979, when I was a Visiting Professor at the Ranchi University Department of Anthropology. During this period I was a guest of Dr Makhan Jha, a very dear friend and a specialist in the study of the sacred complex. Profound gratitude is expressed to him and to his wife, Srimati Uma Jha, for their unflagging hospitality and many acts of kindness, which made my stay in Ranchi pleasant and the planning of this book possible.

The major part of this work was accomplished at the N.K. Bose Memorial Foundation, Varanasi, where I am particularly grateful to my esteemed friends Sri R.L. Maurya and Professor K.P. Mukherjee for undertaking the burden of readying the press copy of the manuscript. Finally, my greatest debt is to my *guru-bhai*, Professor Surajit Sinha, who has been a perennial source of inspiration to most of my writings, including some of the essays presented in this volume, and to my wife Samo who has very generously allowed me to pursue my academic interest unburdened by onerous domestic responsibilities.

Varanasi on the Ganga
August 1982.

BAIDYANATH SARASWATI

ACKNOWLEDGEMENTS

GRATEFUL acknowledgement is made to the American Institute of Indian Studies, especially to its Associate Director, V.R. Nambiar, for making available and granting permission to publish the photographs on the Varanasi ghats and the temples of Dwarka and Rameshwaram, illustrated with this book; also to Dr P.S. Raikar, a close friend of my son, for the photographs on the temples of Goa.

CONTENTS

LIST OF PLATES

INTRODUCTION

THE WESTERN tradition of scholarship, especially the French sociology of religion, has developed a prodigious concept that all known religious beliefs presuppose a classification of all things, real and ideal, into two mutually exclusive and contradictory categories: the sacred and the profane, which cannot be brought together without thereby losing their unique characteristics. Contrary to this notion is the theory of non-dualism (*Advaita*) which has long been established in Indian metaphysical tradition. This book sets out in search of empirical evidence supporting the Indian theory. It has been pointed out that non-dualism is not merely an ontological principle, a logical inference in thought structure, but, in addition, a major value in the social structure and cultural traditions of India. Taking empirical materials into consideration, an attempt has been made in the following pages to develop a theory which implies a continuum between the sacred and the secular.

The central argument in the theory of sacred-secular continuum develops approximately as follows. The continuum theme recurs throughout the Indian scriptural tradition, beginning with the Vedic concept of Man. It finds expressions in such profoundly developed concepts as *purushartha*, *ashrama-dharma*, *jiwana-mukti*, *niskama-karma* etc. which are avowedly the highest ideals of Hindu society. It has been repeatedly stressed that dualism is the product of ignorance (*avidya*) and the salvation of the soul lies in transcending the duality both in thought and in action. Therefore, reaching the highest stage of spirituality, called *turiyatita*, a Hindu ascetic gives up all such distinctions as are socially considered sacred and profane, pure and impure, good and bad. Every householder seeking salvation must also transcend, even though temporarily, the pure-impure boundaries: and hence the rules of cremation in Kashi where the socially untouchable Doms are the custodians of the sacred fire, the rules of pilgrimage to Naimisaranya during which all, regardless of high and low, stand in parity and the rights of periodical entry of the socially impure Mahars in the Shanta Durga temple of Goa. These rules, however, do not move on a merely symbolic level; they are consciously framed and universally accepted as the authentic way of human interaction at the highest state of purity. In the Tantric tradition, the sacred-profane distinction is completely obliterated at the experiential level.

> When the mind goes to rest,
> The bonds of the body are destroyed;
> And when the one flavour of the Innate pours forth,
> There is neither outcaste nor brahmin.

In places of pilgrimage like Kashi the notion of the sacred-secular continuum is actualised in the organization of space, in the performance of rituals, and in the profession of ritual specialists. It is not to say that the sacred-profane opposition is foreign to Indian ideals and experience. In fact, this has been an important criterion in the organization of Indian social life. But what makes the Indian tradition intrinsically different from all other traditions is the perception of the Absolute, the Supreme. Brahma, in Indian tradition is the *coincidentia oppositorum.* This character of Brahma—the falling together of all opposites—is also the highest ideal of Man because, after all, Man's ultimate goal is to become *brahmalina*, to merge with the Absolute. In order that the ideal be realised, appropriate canons of behaviour have been prescribed at critical moments in religious life. Thus, in the final analysis, what appears significant in Indian sacred tradition is *not* the opposition but the continuum between the sacred and the secular.

This idea is further supported by empirical data on the cultural foundations of the sacred. Hindu pilgrims belonging to three cultural traditions, namely; oral, textual and transcendental, treat the sacred complex of Kashi differently, according to the norms of their respective tradition, and yet share in common the Indian vision of the Truth. Here again, the pilgrims of the three traditions form a continuum. All the three different notions of the sacred—the malevolent sacred, identified by OCT; the benevolent sacred, conceived by TCT; and a third dimension of the sacred, repudiating both the malevolent and the benevolent, envisioned by Tran CT—from a real set of religious phenomen.a

Interpretations of poetry and pilgrimage point out to the same principle. In almost all traditional cultures the proper context of both poetry and pilgrimage is the sacred. The sacred journey is performed at several different levels of diversities—diversity of categories, diversity of performances, diversity of performers, and diversity of regional cultures—and yet there is, in Indian tradition, an overall unity of beliefs and behaviour at all levels. The point of unity is the point of convergence of all beliefs as "part truths", originating in the religious experience of Man. In both primitive and classical cultures the proper context of poetry is the sacred. The primitive cultures make no big difference between poetic language and the everyday language. All classical cultures composed only religious poetry, at least basically. Nothing in Hindu classical culture, for instance, can be called truly secular poetry—even the highly erotic poetry relates to the gods. Such a comprehension of the totally sacralized human existence is obviously incompatible with a Durkheimian theory of binary opposition treating the sacred and the secular as mutually exclusive and contradictory categories.

What might appear provocative in this book are the assumptions that in the Indian belief system the central aspect of ritual is its cosmological function: preserving the universe, and the religious life negates social life, destroys cultural boundaries and librates every person individually. These are transanthropological assumptions which have been discussed here only briefly and which I wish to take up at some length in a later work.

However, my chief concern in this volume is to highlight the Indian vision of the sacred and thereby to offer some guidance in thinking about the sacred-secular continuum.

Sketch map of India showing the location of Tirthas

PART ONE

1

THE CONCEPT OF THE SACRED

THE THEORY OF BINARY OPPOSITION

THE NOTION holy (sacred) perhaps is the best keyword of religion. N. Söderblom was the first to draw attention to the significance of this term (Bleeker 1963). Rudolf Otto (1923) made this notion popular through his famous book *Das Heilige* (The Sacred), published in 1917. His main assertion was that the sacred is a category *sui generis*, i.e., it differs in nature and quality from all that is human, secular or *profane*. Otto's notion of this sacred-profane distinction has found assent both in the phenomenology of religion and in the history of religions. The sociologists of religion have also made use of his ideas liberally and have introduced many other opposed groups or classes traditionally characterized as *pure* and *impure*, *real* and *unreal*, *good* and *bad*. Several scholars have contributed to this notion of duality in religious phenomena.

Mircea Eliade (1957, 1961), one of the most outstanding historians of religions, has perceived the sacred-profane polarity as: The first possible definition of the *sacred* is that it is *the opposite of the profane*. Man becomes aware of the sacred because it manifests itself, shows itself as something wholly different from the profane—the manifestation of something of a wholly different order, a reality that does not belong to our world, in objects that are an integral part of our natural "profane" world. *Sacred* and *profane* are two modes of being in the world, two existential situations assumed by man in the course of his history. For religious man, space is not homogeneous; some parts of space are qualitatively different from others. There is a sacred space; there are other spaces that are not sacred. Every sacred space implies a hierophany, an irruption, of the sacred that results in detaching a territory from the surrounding cosmic milieu and making it qualitatively different. Time too, like space, is neither homogeneous nor continuous. On the one hand there are the intervals of a sacred time, the time of festivals; on the other there is profane time, ordinary temporal duration, in which acts without religious meaning have their setting. In the festival the sacred dimension of life is recovered. Religious man assumes a particular and characteristic mode of existence in the world, and always believes that there is an absolute reality, the *sacred* which transcends this world but manifests itself in this world, thereby sanctifying it and making it real.

Emile Durkheim (1912, 1961), one of the founders of modern sociology, has thus defined and characterized the sacred: All known religious beliefs, whether simple or complex, present one common characteristic: they presuppose a classification of all the things, real and ideal, of which men think, into two classes or opposed groups, generally designated by two distinct terms—*profane* and *sacred.* This division of the world into two domains, the one containing all that is sacred, the other all that is profane, is the distinctive trait of religious thought. Sacred things are considered superior in dignity and power to profane things and particularly to man, when he is only a man and has nothing sacred about him. But if a purely hierarchic distinction is a criterium at once too general and too imprecise, there is nothing left with which to characterize the sacred in its relation to the profane except their heterogeneity. However, this heterogeneity is sufficient to characterize this classification of things and to distinguish it from all others, because it is very particular—*it is absolute.* In all the history of human thought there exists no other example of two categories of things so profoundly differentiated or so radically opposed to one another. The sacred and the profane have always and everywhere been conceived by the human mind as two distinct classes, as two worlds between which there is nothing in common. The forces which play in one are not simply those which are met with in the other, but a little stronger—they are of different sort. This heterogeneity is even so complete that it frequently degenerates into a veritable antagonism. The two worlds are not only conceived of as separate, but as even hostile and jealous rivals of each other. The sacred thing is *par excellence* that which the profane should not touch, and cannot touch with impunity. The two classes cannot even approach each other and keep their own nature at the same time. The real characteristic of religious phenomena is that they always suppose a bipartite division of the whole universe, known and knowable, into two classes which embrace all that exists, but which radically exclude each other. Sacred things are those which the interdictions protect and isolate; profane things, those to which these interdictions are applied and which must remain at a distance from the first.

Roger Caillois (1959), a distinguished French sociologist, has underlined the following characteristics of the sacred: Every religious conception of the universe implies a distinction between the sacred and the profane and is opposed to the world in which the believer freely attends to his business and engages in activity heedless of his salvation. The domain of the sacred is one in which he is paralyzed in turn by fear and by hope. These two worlds, the sacred and the profane, are rigorously defined only in relation to each other. They are mutually exclusive and contradictory. The sacred is related as a common property, solid or ephemeral, to certain objects (the instruments of the cult), to certain beings (kings, priests), to certain places (temple, church, mountain peak), to certain times (Sunday, Easter, Christmas, etc.). There is nothing that cannot become its resting place. The sacred is not something that can be taken away. It is a quality that things do not possess in themselves—a mysterious aura that has been added to things. The sacred being, the consecrated object, can in no way be modified in its appearance. Nevertheless it is transformed in moving from person to person. It stimulates feelings of terror and veneration; it becomes "taboo". Contact with it becomes dangerous. The sacred is always more or less what one cannot approach without dying. It is no less necessary to protect the sacred from any taint of the profane.

The profane, in effect, alters its essence, causes it to lose its unique quality—the void created by the impression of the formidable and fleeting power it contains. The profane, in relationship to the sacred, simply endows it with negative properties. The profane, in comparison, seems as poor and bereft of existence as nothingness is to being. Watertight compartments separate the sacred from the profane. On the other hand, they are both necessary for the evolution of life—one, as the environment within which life unfolds; the other, as the inexhaustible source that creates, sustains and renews it.

The foregoing excerpts should serve to underline the essential duality of the religious phenomena broadly defined in terms of the sacred—profane opposition. It may now be pointed out that even within the sacred itself some sort of duality has been ascribed. Durkheim has described the ambiguity of the sacred as : The pure and the impure are not two separate classes, but two varieties of the same class, which includes all sacred things. There are two sorts of sacredness, the propitious and the unpropitious, and not only is there no break of continuity between these two opposed forms, but also one object may pass from the one to the other without changing its nature. The pure is made out of the impure, and reciprocally. It is in the possibility of these transmutations that the ambiguity of the sacred consists.

Caillois has analysed the ambiguity of the sacred more explicitly. He digresses on the various aspects of the problem, as appears from the captions of his book, namely, Purity and Intermixture; The Pure and the Impure: Equivocal Forces; Sanctity and Defilement; The Sacred Dialectic; Acquisition and Loss of Purity, Precautions Against Defilement and Sanctity; The Polarity of the Sacred, Opposition of the Two Poles of the Sacred, The Reversibility of Pure and Impure. The Elimination of Inexpiable Defilement; Cohesion and Dissolution; Social Distribution of the Pure and the Impure, Localization of the Pure and Impure, Purity and Impurity: Autonomous States, Evolution of the Concepts of the Pure and Impure, Profane and Sacred. Here Caillois makes an interesting assertion: Everything in the universe is susceptible to dichotomization and can thus symbolize the varied, inter-related, and antagonistic manifestations of the pure and the impure. Living energies and the powers of death are joined to form the positive and negative poles of the religious world. To the former, belong the clearness and dryness of day; to the latter, the darkness and dampness of night. The East and the South seem to be the seat of qualities and growth (they cause the sun to rise and become warmer); and the West and the North are the habitat of the powers of perdition and ruin (they cause the star of life to descend and become extinguished). High and low become distinguishable—the sky serves as the abode of gods, and the subterranean world is reserved for the dark abode in which death's sway is absolute. At this point Caillois refers to Robert Hertz who set up this dichotomy in terms of *right* and *left* applied in ritual, in the practice of divination, in customs and in beliefs.

What transpires from the foregoing allusions is the leading theory of binary opposition as applied to all religious phenomena. It may be underlined that this theory has originated in the Western tradition of scholarship (particularly the French tradition) and that it has been derived from the analysis of data mainly on primitive religions. However, this is now being widely applied to more developed religions and complex societies.

INTERPRETATION OF HINDU SOCIETY AND RELIGION

Religion pervades the entire social structure. Hence, the principles applied to a religious system are applicable to the society which upholds it. The theory of binary opposition of the sacred and the profane has been applied to the interpretation of Hindu society and religion. The Western scholars were baffled by the purity-pollution behaviour of common Hindus—the phenomenon so apparently intricate and elaborate as they never had envisaged or experienced in the context of their own society. Their basic approach to the understanding of Hindu society, therefore, revolved through the ideology of "purity and pollution". The Indian scholars have, faithfully followed the path of their Western gurus.

The theory that runs through the main currents of today's

dialogue on Hinduism and the Indian caste system is what might be called the Dumontian theory. Louis Dumont (1970) has observed that the universal human opposition of the sacred and the profane is substituted in the context of Hindu social relations by the opposition of the pure and the impure, and that the caste system is based upon the hierarchical opposition of the pure and the impure. For Dumont, hierarchy is purely a matter of religious value. He defines hierarchical relation as a relation between the larger and the smaller or more precisely between that which encompasses and that which is encompassed. He further brings into relief a number of binary distinctions to describe the underlying structure of Hindu thought—the opposition between the world renouncer (*Sannyasi*) and the man-in-the world, between priesthood and possession, between (religious) status and (temporal) power, and between pure and impure.

Several scholars have contributed to this model of binary opposition. Veena Das (1973, 1976, 1977) has made a significant analysis of society and cosmos in Hinduism. She argues that in Hindu ritual and belief the internal ordering of the sacred is in terms of life and death. The cosmic world is divided into two parts: the sacred associated with life and the sacred associated with death. While dealing with the life-preserving aspects of the sacred cosmos, the state of purity is considered appropriate. The state of impurity, on the other hand, marks off those situations which are liminal in the sense that the individual experiences his social world as separated from the cosmic. Das observes one more distinction: the rituals pertaining to the passage of time (the morning and evening oblations), the rituals dealing with initiation, pregnancy, childbirth and marriage are those in which the right side of the body predominates; on the other hand, the left side of the body predominates in rituals of cremation, in rites to ghosts, demons, in rites to ancestors and serpents. Thus, the distinction between auspicious and inauspicious, and between life and death is made through the construction of ritual space and the use of four cardinal points of the compass.

One of Das's students, Meena Kaushik (1979), has studied the Doms of Kashi who are traditionally the custodians of the sacred fire which Hindus of all categories use for the purpose of cremation. She has demonstrated with considerable clarity how the opposition between 'hot' and 'cold', as used in the Dom system of thought, brings to the fore a classificatory system which associates life with 'heat' and death with 'cold'. Earlier, Lawrence Babb (1970) had brought into relief how the hot-cold opposition in the Javara ceremony of the Chhattisgarhis in Madhya Pradesh relates to a cultural principle that hotness and coldness are fundamental properties of existence. Meena Kaushik makes an interesting analysis of the Dom's death ritual complex in terms of four symbolic codes, namely, lateral symbolism, spatial symbolism, culinary symbolism, and acoustic symbolism.

Lateral symbolism

The human body is here being divided into two equal and mirror opposites—the right and the left. This division is dramatically expressed through the rituals relating to life and death. For instance, the funeral pyre is always lit with the left hand, and the chief mourner offers the left shoulder to carry the corpse. The right hand, on the contrary, is used to offer oblations to the gods and also when performing rituals associated with sacredness of life, like marriage.

The spatial code

The code divides the universe into the four major cardinal points—North, South, East and West. The Hindu conceives of the North and the East as associated with the realm of gods, good sacredness, and the right. South and West are associated with ancestors, 'left-handed' sects and the left. The corpse is placed along the North-South axis with the head towards the south. Offerings to ghost and demons are also placed in the southern direction. In contrast to this, in marriage the spatial points are North and East. The bride and the groom must face the East and offer oblations with the right hand.

Culinary code

A number of binary distinctions order the culinary domain. It is through the ordering of opposition like *kutcha-pukka*, *taja-basi*, *sucha-jutha*, and *sabut-tuta* that food offerings are made to gods.

The distinction between 'hot' and 'cold' is another important ordering principle. Heat is associated with life and death with cold. The *preta* is always offered cold food. This is opposed to hot food that the living partake. In death, the domestic hearth is broken, or allowed to lie cold. This symbolises a loss of life.

The acoustic code

It is expressed in the opposition between sound and silence. It marks out the distinctive stages of the ritual complex. Among the Doms, the corpse is carried to the cremation ghat accompanied by drummers and loud weeping is permitted at the cremation, though after the water is offered to the *preta* it must cease. The *preta* must not be disturbed in his journey to the world of the *pitar*.

In his monumental work on Hindu Gaya, a celebrated place of pilgrimage, Vidyarthi (1978) introduces the concept of *sacred complex* formed of three inter-related phenomena: (1) sacred geography, (2) sacred performances, and (3) sacred specialists. He describes the sacred geography of Gaya in terms of sacred centre, sacred cluster and sacred segments. A sacred centre represents a single spot where a sacred performance takes place. Such a sacred centre may be variously located. It may be isolated. Then a sacred centre may be in a cluster of many other sacred centres in its adjacent neighbourhood. To denote such a combination of sacred centres around a dominant sacred centre, the term sacred cluster has been used. On another local and organizational level two or more clusters forming a continuous segment may be termed the sacred segment. The sacred performances are linked with the sacred centres. These may be analysed into floral offerings, meditational exercises, oblations, libations, artistic performances, and religious donations. The various types of sacred specialists are connected, on the one hand, with the sacred centres and performances there, and, on the other, with the sacrificers (*yajmans*)—the pilgrims. Among the sacred specialists are mentioned temple priests, florists, drummers, barbers, pandas, gumastas and such other functionaries professionally associated with sacred performances. Vidyarthi's model has been applied to various centres of pilgrimages[1] in India and Nepal—also in tribal contexts—and most of his followers and students have asserted that the concept of sacred complex with its attending terminology has a much wider applicability and that it reflects one of the important dimensions of Indian civilization. It may be stated at this point that nowhere Vidyarthi has defined the term *sacred,* yet there is no ambiguity in his treatment of the term. The term *sacred* has been used precisely in the sense of Durkheimian and Dumontian distinction as the opposite of the profane, that is the opposite of the secular. In point of functional and cultural importance the city of Gaya has been demarcated into two zones: the sacred and the secular. The sacred-secular distinction recurs throughout the book: sacred zone—secular zone, sacred place—secular place, sacred service—secular service, sacred specialists—secular agencies, sacred performances—secular jobs, sacred intelligentsia—secular scholars. All these allusions show that the sacred-secular dichotomy has been maintained with unfaltering clarity.

Thus, what has come out from the foregoing discussion is a semantic system which constitutes the various binary oppositions between the sacred and the profane, the sacred and the secular, the pure and the impure, the auspicious and the inauspicious, the good sacred and the bad sacred, the auspicious sacred and the inauspicious sacred, and the various symbolic codes of hot and cold, up and down, right and left, living and dead, cardinal points of space, sound and silence, and so on and so forth. Most scholars have used these terms and categories in the Durkheimian sense, that is, as "absolute" and "radically opposed" and their inter-relationship as a dominant ideological framework for the study of religions. In the main stream of Indian sociological and social anthropological traditions this framework of religions research has already acquired a place of heuristic importance.

SACRED-SECULAR CONTINUUM

I should now take you to another stream of thought which signifies a break from the main tradition.

Power on par with purity

Let me revert to the three basic assumptions in Dumont's interpretation of Hinduism and the caste system: First, purity-impurity opposition is central to the caste system; second, hierarchy and separation are the basic aspects of opposition between purity and impurity; and third, power is subordinate to religious status. Those who have contended against this theory hold that Dumont's assumptions are based on a wrong perception of Hindu ideology: some have come out with empirical findings that go against these assumptions.

For instance, Wadley's (1977) study of beliefs of the Hindu peasants about the nature of their deities and the deities relationship to men, shows that *purity* and *power* are inseparable categories. She says: rather than agreeing that purity or the principle of pure-impure is dominant in Hindu society (as Dumont proposes), I contend that purity and power are inseparable factors of any idea of being or action in Hindu thought. Brahmins are the most powerful beings and the most pure. Even the gods' powers are connected with their purity: those with the highest influence tend to be the most pure. Both power and purity are used jointly in determining hierarchical relationships. Thus any being is at one and the same time purity and power, and that way action changes both purity and power.

This identification of purity and power is evident also in the work of L.K. Mahapatra. Mahapatra (1977) illustrates how god-king and temple-palace are inseparable categories in Orissa. The king of Puri is called *Thakur-Raja* (God-King) and *Chalanti-Visnu* (mobile Visnu). The pilgrims used to have *darshana* (audience) of the king before proceeding to the temple of Jagannath. They would not enter the palace with leather foot-wear, as in temple. The king and the god underwent similar rituals at the time of waking up, bathing, receiving presents, eating breakfast, putting on clothes, giving audience, making offerings, and other daily rituals. The author concludes that the god-king combination is at the heart of the state and society in Orissa.

Thus, both Wadley and Mahapatra have demonstrated that in Hindu society, power is treated on par with purity, rather than, as Dumont would have it, as distinct from and encompassed by purity.

Man-God continuum

In an interesting article, Aiyappan (1977) tests a non-dualistic proposition that there is a continuum between gods and intermediate levels and humans. In support of this proposition he presents the data on ancestral cults and myths of the matrilineal Kurichiya tribals of Wynad in Kerala. His analysis shows that while only some ancestral spirits return to guide the living, the line between such spirits and intermediate gods in obliterated in time. Myths record seven deities as deified humans. Aiyappan argues that Shankar's *Advaita* (non-dualistic or monistic Hindu theology, which views the human spirit and the divine as identical—as a unity), and the concept of *avatar* (the incarnations of gods as human beings or animals) are the aspects of the man-God continuum which is central and crucial in Hindu religion and mythology. He posits an interesting hypothesis, that the germ of the idea of monism, namely, the continuity of man with God, is likely to be found among the primitive sub-stratum of Indian population.

God-man relationship figures also in Wadley's (1977) structural analysis of power in Hindu ideology and practice. The author explains the presence of equivalence in God-man relationship: Faith and service on the part of the worshippers are reciprocal on the part of the deity by mercy and boons. The transactions represented by these two sets of terms mediate between man and gods, as do the opposite transactions represented by disrespectful or wrong act by men and anger or revenge by gods.

Khare (1977) makes an interesting analysis of prestations and prayers. He argues that prayers essentially follow a logical paradigm that is characteristic of social prestations, and this is particularly true for the devotional prayers of Hinduism. These prayers are essentially based on the premise 'give-and-take' with an explicit idea of both quality and quantity of exchange between the deity and the devotee. The person who says prayers offers 'something' to his deity, which in return, reciprocates. One static view is that the deity always gives and the devotee always receives. However, on closer inspection, the feature of reciprocity comes to the fore; a deity does not 'give' without receiving something from the devotee. Further, while in a religious sense, a direction is built into prayers (God always gives more than a human can hope to reciprocate), in actuality, the reverse is more true, where a devotee prays whether his deity immediately answers him or not. But this is true only to an extent. A temple priest once told the author: Who will pray if it is not answered at all, or more accurately, if there is no idea (or hope) that it is to be answered, even in the remotest way, in the remotest time. Thus the principle of reciprocity is at work in prayers, as in social prestations.

Roy-Burman (1974) makes a distinction between the Christian and the Hindu concept of the sacred. In Christianity he says, terrestrial life is inextricably linked up with sin, with the loss of paradise, and the goal of human life is the expiation of sin, the regaining of the paradise. Secular is, therefore, synonymous with profane, and is the obvious anti-thesis of the sacred. But in Hindu tradition sacred is not external to the secular; it is the inherent potency of the secular.

In my rejoinder (Saraswati 1974) to Roy-Burman's interpretation of the Hindu concept of sacred, I had said that in Brahminic sacerdotal tradition man is not a despised being; he is not inherently subservient to God. The examples of the Vedic *rishis* and the Brahminic ritual craft indicate that by means of *tapas* man has been 'creating' sacred and by means of rituals he has been reversing the course of the sacred—the will of gods. It was only at the later phase of Hinduism—its encounter with Islam and Christianity and the resultant syncretism—that a Hindu began to rely heavily and helplessly on the will of gods.

The Hindu view of human glory is reflected best in the Vedic vision of Man. The glorious Man of the Veda is different from the Biblical man burdened with a guilt complex. The Vedic man is 'powerful'. Although he invokes gods and asks for happiness, health, wealth, prosperity and progeny, his invocation has the force of a commission. Unlike the man of

Christian, Islamic and other traditions, he does not seek mercy and judgement, he asks gods fearlessly to perform their respective function. And "the function of God is not to judge but to protect, to help man thrive and flourish". The Vedic man desires to be endowed with 'unlimited powers' and aspires to be invested with the glory of gods. This is so clearly stated in the following excerpts from the Atharva Veda.[2]

1. May the splendour of an elephant,
        the greatest of all creatures,
        may that great glory,
    which was born from the Boundless, now be diffused,
    gods together have bestowed it upon me.
2. On this splendour have all the powers of heaven
        concentrated their thought.
    May those gods who nourish all life on earth
        anoint me with splendour!
3. That splendour that resides in the elephant, in a king
        among men, or within the waters,
    with which gods in the beginning came to godhood,
    with that same splendour make me splendid, O Lord.

(*AV III*, 22)

1. With the splendour that resides in a lion, a tiger,
        an adder, the fire,
        Brahman, the sun,
    may that blessed Goddess who gave birth to Indra
    now come to us, endowed with splendour!
2. With the splendour that resides in an elephant,
        a leopard,
        in gold, in the waters,
        in cattle and in men,
    may that blessed Goddess who gave birth to Indra
    now come to us, endowed with splendour!
3. With the splendour that resides in a chariot, in dice,
        in a strong bull, in wind,
        in rain and in thunder,
    may that blessed Goddess who gave birth to Indra
    now come to us, endowed with splendour!

4. With the splendour that resides in a noble, a drumbeat,
an arrow's flight, a man's shout,
a mettlesome horse,
may that blessed Goddess who gave birth to Indra
now come to us, endowed with splendour!

(*AV VI*, 38)

Raimundo (1977) offers a meaningful interpretation of the Vedic view of man-God relationship. Reflecting upon the famous *Purusa Sukta*—The Primordial Man—he says: God, man, and the universe are correlates. God without man is nothing, literally "no thing". Man without God is exclusively a "thing", not a person, not a really human being, while the world, the cosmos, without man and God is "anything", without consistency and being; it is sheer unexisting chaos. The three are constitutively connected. Nothing separates man from God. There is neither intermediary nor barrier between them. The primordial man is the living expression of the ontonomic man, that total reality of which we are a reflection. God is not totally other than man, nor is the world an entity utterly foreign to man. Man is more than a single individual and more than the sum of all individuals. Without this internal and constitutive link with the whole of reality, and life of contemplation would become sheer egoism or a kind of spiritual narcissism. Authentic spiritual life or *dharmic* existence amounts to assimilating in one's self the maximum possible of the *purusa* condition of reality. *Purusa* is not only the cosmic man; it is also the personal aspect of the whole of reality. The *purusa* sacrifices himself by dismembering himself and scattering around the necessary number of portions for the completion of the work of creation. He performs an act of self-immolation so that the universe may come into being. From this sacrifice offered completely, that is, from the limbs of the Cosmic Man, come all things both animate and inanimate: animals of every type; liturgical formula; the four castes of men; the cosmic powers. The Cosmic Man is the total sacrifice. By sacrifice creation reverts to the man. The sacrifice of the Cosmic Man signifies divine transcendence investing humanity. This universal sacrifice possesses a two-fold dynamism, for it includes a sacramental downward movement of the All toward the earth and a sacrificial upward movement of the world toward the All; these two aspects are inseparable, one from the other, precisely because of the unity of the integral sacrifice.

We must recall at this point that the above description of the primordial sacrifice does not relate to historical beings or a temporal origin of things, it rather explains an ontological principle. But what is significant about this principle is that it is extended to non-ontological principle and practice, as in Hindu ritual craft. Sacrifice (*yajna*) is the supreme principle and practice of classical Brahminism. By sacrifice man obtains both material benefits and immortality, acquires wisdom, health, wealth and progeny, establishes social relationships, and communicates and collaborates with gods.

Continuum at empirical level

I have discussed elsewhere (Saraswati 1975) that the sacred and the secular are dialectically rather than dichotomously related. My basic assumption is that the sacred-secular continuum is not merely an ideational principle, a philosophical speculation, it is an empirical reality that can be observed at critical moments in life as also in the organization of sacred traditions. In a sacred place like Kashi, in the organization of its space, in the performance of rituals, and in the profession of ritual specialists, it is almost impossible to make a clear-cut distinction between the sacred and the secular. In the drudgery of social life one may find certain diacritical marks artificially dividing people into high and low, pure and impure, sacred and profane, but as one mounts higher and higher in the spiritual disciplining of life (*sadhana*) these differences begin to evaporate. The purity-pollution boundaries have been repeatedly transgressed by saints and mystics, and sacred laws have been prescribed to rise above the petty differences in social life. This is the spiritual necessity to every Hindu who wishes to be truly liberated. When a Brahmin--the tallest and the purest in the society—comes to Kashi for the cremation of his deceased kinsman he asks for the sacred fire from the socially untouchable Doms, who are its traditional custodian. Without this 'sacred fire' the deceased cannot attain *moksha*—the supreme sacred. From such examples, how can one dichotomize "sacred" and "secular" or "sacred" and "profane" in the Durkheimian sense? Indeed, they are the two sides of the same coin—the difference lies in the perception of the observer, depending from what angle he looks at it. Nothing solely sacred or solely profane exists in the common experience of life, or in the ultimate analysis of things.

NOTES

1. For instance, Janakpur (M. Jha, 1971, *The Sacred Complex of Janakpur*, Allahabad); Kashi [B.N. Saraswati, 1971, Sacred complex in Kashi. In Surajit Sinha (ed.), *Research Projects in Social Anthropology*, Calcutta; L.P. Vidyarthi, B.N. Saraswati and M. Jha, 1979, *The Sacred Complex of Kashi*, Concept, New Delhi]; Rajgir [R.K. Sinha, 1971, Rajgir and its People, *Journal of Social Research*, 1971, 14(1): 68-75]; Deoghar (S. Narayan, 1972, *The Sacred Complex of Deoghar and Rajgir*, Concept, New Delhi, 1983); Tarkeshwar [P. Chakrabarti, 1973, Some observations on the pilgrims and their pilgrimages: A case study of Tarkeshwar, *Human Events*, 1973, 7(7): 17-20]; Dwarka [V.S. Upadhyay, 1974, The sacred geography of Dwarka, *Journal of Social Research*, 1974, 17(1): 42-8]; Gupta-Kashi [M. Mahapatra, 1974, The sacred geography of Gupta-Kashi, *Journal of Social Research*, 1974, 17(1): 75-87]; Rameshwaram and Tirupati [K.N. Sahay, 1974, The sacred geography of Rameshwaram and Tirupati, *Journal of Social Research*, 1974, 17(1): 49-51]; Bakreshwar [R.M. Sarkar, 1976, Study of sacred complex and the Bakreshwar temple, *Indian Anthropologist*, 1976, 6(2): 17-26]; Madhi [S.K. Huble, T. Vetschera and S. Khome, 1976. The sacred complex of Madhi, *Man in India*, 1976, 56(3): 237-62].
2. These extracts have been quoted from Raimundo Panikkar's celebrated work (1977), *The Vedic Experience: Mantramanjari.*

REFERENCES

Aiyappan, A., 1977. Deified men and humanized gods: some folk bases of Hindu theology. In Kenneth David (ed.), *The new Wind: Changing Identities in South Asia*, The Hague, 1977, 95-104.

Babb, Lawrence A., 1970. The food of gods in Chhattisgarh: Some structural features of Hindu ritual, *Southwestern Journal of Anthropology*, 26: 287-304.

Bleeker, C.J., 1963. *The Sacred Bridge: Researches into the Nature and Structure of Religion*, Leiden, Netherlands.

Caillois, Roger, 1959. *Man and the Sacred* (Tr. by Meyer Barash), Illinois.

Das, Veena, 1973. The categorization of space in Hindu ritual. In R.K. Jain (ed.), *Text and Context: The Social Anthropology of Tradition*, Philadelphia, 1973, 9-27.

Das, Veena, 1976. The uses of liminality: society and cosmos in Hinduism, *Contributions to Indian Sociology* (N.S.), 10(2), 246-63.

Das, Veena, 1977. *Structure and Cognition: Aspects of Hindu Caste and Ritual*, Delhi.

Dumont, Louis, 1970. *Homo Hierarchicus: The Caste System and its Implications*, London.

Durkheim, Emile, 1961. *The Elementary Forms of the Religious Life*, New York.

Eliade, Mircea, 1961. *The Sacred and the Profane: The Nature of Religion*, New York.

Kaushik, Meena, 1979. *Religion and Social Structure: A Case Study of the Doms of Banaras* (Ph.D dissertation, The University of Delhi), Delhi.

Khare, R.S., 1977. Prestations and prayers: Two homologous systems in nothern India. In Kenneth David (ed.), *The New Wind: Changing Identities in South Asia*, The Hague, 1977, 105-32.

Mahapatra, L.K., 1977. Gods kings and the caste system in India. In Kenneth David (ed.), *The New Wind: Changing Identities in South Asia*, The Hague, 1977, 159-78.

Otto, Rudolf, 1923. *The Idea of the Holy*, London.

Panikkar, Raimundo, 1977. *The Vedic Experience: Mantramanjari: An Anthology of the Vedas for Modern Man and Contemporary Celebration*, Berkeley, Los Angeles.

Roy-Burman, B.K., 1974. Structure of the sacred in ritual terracottas, *Man in India*, 54(1).

Saraswati, Baidyanath, 1974. Structure of the sacred in ritual terracotta: A rejoinder, *Man in India*, 54(1), 85-89.

Saraswati, Baidyanath, 1975. *Kashi: Myth and Reality of a Classical Cultural Tradition*, Simla.

Vidyarthi, L.P., 1978. *The Sacred Complex in Hindu Gaya*, Concept, New Delhi.

Wadley, Susan, 1977. Power in Hindu ideology and practice. In Kenneth David (ed.), *The New Wind: Changing Identities in South Asia*, The Hague, 1977, 133-58.

2

THE SACRED COMPLEX IN INDIAN CULTURAL TRADITIONS

THERE are three principal modes of transmission of knowledge in Indian civilization: (1) the oral-observational mode, followed in *laukic vidya*, (2) the textual mode, employed in *apara vidya*, and (3) the transcendental mode, adopted in *para vidya*. These modes of transmission have shaped three cultural traditions so distinctly and intrinsically that each adopts one of these as *the essential mode of survival* and changes effectively when the mode is changed.

Adopting this scheme, all the varieties of Indian cultural traditions may be grouped under three main traditions, termed as (1) Oral Cultural Tradition (OCT), (2) Textual Cultural Tradition (TCT), and (3) Transcendental Cultural Tradition (TranCT). Following Sanskrit terminology, these may be called *laukic sanskriti*, *apara sanskriti*, and *para sanskriti*. I have described them elsewhere as *laukic* culture, *shastric* (*shastriya*) culture, and *naivritic* culture respectively (Saraswati 1970). In the following pages these traditions will be referred to in their abbreviated forms as OCT, TCT and TranCT.

According to Vidyarthi (1961), *The Sacred Complex in Hindu Gaya* is composed of (1) sacred geography, (2) sacred performances, and (3) sacred specialists. The sacred geography has been further classified into zones, segments, and clusters of sacred centres. It may be pointed out that this classification of the sacred phenomena is applicable not only to Gaya, but also to many other sacred places of Hindu pilgrimage. Both Vidyarthi (1961) and Cohn and Marriott (1958) have considered these places and the networks of pilgrimages functionally important in the integration of Indian civilization. These authors have also shown that the sacred centres of pilgrimages are the centres of civilization where pilgrims from different regions of India, from different levels of culture, interact. But, do these heterogeneous pilgrims who interact in a sacred complex share in common the Brahminic concept of the sacred which has originally laid the foundation of these centres? Do all of them interact fully and equally with the sacred phenomena operating at a sacred centre? In Semitic religions, all those who interact in a place of pilgrimage, say Mecca or Jerusalem, may belong to diverse linguistic regions and cultural strata, yet they participate equally in the sacred performances. This does not seem to be true with the Hindu places of pilgrimage which yet serve importantly in the integration of diverse cultural traditions into a common bond of civilization. What are then the modalities of integration in sacred and secular life?

To answer these questions, we shall examine in the following pages whether the pilgrims belonging to the three cultural traditions, mentioned above, participate equally in the sacred complex at both behavioural and ideational levels. Thus, for instance, whether a peasant potter belonging to Oral Cultural Tradition (OCT), a Brahmin belonging to Textural Cultural Tradition (TCT), and a *Dandi Sannyasi* belonging to Transcendental Cultural Tradition (TranCT) equally share the sacred complex in a pilgrim centre, say in Kashi?

PILGRIMS' PARTICIPATION IN THE SACRED COMPLEX

In Kashi, it is said, there are thirtythree hundred million shrines and half a million images. There are, at least, three hundred-and-thirty living temples dedicated to various gods and goddesses whose references occur in the *Kashi Khanda* of the *Skanda Purana*. Although it may not be possible for all the pilgrims to visit all the shrines and to worship all the images, their ideal and actual performances are defined by their traditions. For instance, while the pilgrims belonging to TCT are ideally required to worship, at least, all gods and goddesses referred to in the *Kashi Khanda*, there is no such ritual necessity for the pilgrims belonging to OCT.

A potter pilgrim feels contented by visiting the main Vishwanath temple. His Brahmin guide may, however, take him to a few other temples but that does not form an essential part of his pilgrimage. What is important for him is to have a *darshana* of God Vishwanath and a bath in the Ganga whereby all his sins will be blotted out. But he will make, on his own, a special pilgrimage to the non-Brahminic shrines of deified heroes, known as *birs* such as Agivabir and Lahurabir and bathe in the *Krimi-kunda*, a sacred tank located in Keenaramka Astar. This he does for his general well-being, to get rid of his chronic disease, if any, or to have an offspring. He will also pay a visit to Augharki Takiya to be blessed by the *aughar*, and to drink sacred water from the well which has the power to heal various kinds of diseases. He will perform *pindadana* ritual at the ghats under the direction of a Brahmin priest, and although he will himself perform no ritual in a temple he may bring flowers, sweets, incense, and such other objects as the priest may demand from him to offer to the deity on his behalf. For, he is traditionally entitled only for the *darshana*. But when he visits Agiyabir he himself offers wine and *ganja* (hashish), and sacrifices a fowl or a goat. There he may also take the help of a non-Brahmin priest of the shrine, but he can do it there even without the priest.

Thus, the potter's participation in the Brahminic sacred complex in Kashi is minimal and peripheral. Where he interacts more freely and closely are the places which have no textual reference that makes Kashi an important place of all-Hindu pilgrimage.

A Brahmin pilgrim is ideally required to visit all the shrines mentioned in the *Skanda Purana*, as also all the new temples that have been consecrated according to the *shastras*. He is also required to circumambulate on the sacred path, known as *panchakroshi parikrama*, which runs around the sacred city within the radius of five miles. There is another route of circumambulation which encompasses the adjoining holy places connected with the Kashi-kshetra. This is called *chaurasikroshi parikrama*, which covers the holy Vindhyachal-kshetra, to which a devout pilgrim traverses on foot. The Brahmin pilgrim is also expected to bathe at all the eightyone ghats on the Ganga and in various *kundas* or sacred wells and tanks. There is a long list of elaborate rituals which the *shastras* have enjoined on him to perform at various shrines located in the Kashi-kshetra.

For each ancient place of Hindu pilgrimage there is a written text, called *Mahatmya*, which draws its sources essentially from some of the *Puranas*. It serves as a guide-book of pilgrimage. There are two such books, *Kashi Mahatmya* and *Kashi Yatrà*, published by Sri Venkateshwar Steam Press, Bombay. Both these books have listed the prescribed rituals and the way of life to be followed during pilgrimage to Kashi. But it is extremely difficult, if not impossible, to follow all that is prescribed in the *mahatmya grantha*. Hence, pilgrimages are performed, according to one's ability and convenience, by concentrating on one or more than one segments of the *kshetra*. According to the *Skanda Purana*, the Kashi-kshetra is divided into three *khandas* or segments, known as (1) Visheshwara-khanda, (2) Kedara-khanda, and (3) Omkara-khanda. Since Visheshwara is the presiding God of the *kshetra*, all must pay a visit to his shrine. It may be pointed out that there is no hierarchy among the sacred shrines of *shastric* origin. Nevertheless, it is true that while some of them are regularly visited by a large number of pilgrims, others are less popular for various historical and organizational reasons.

To these shrines, the Brahmin pilgrim pays a visit according to his ability and convenience. But, besides the main Visheshwara shrine, which is a must for everyone, he visits, at least, one shrine from among each of the important groups of gods and goddesses mentioned in the *Skanda Purana* such as Shiva, Mangala Gauri, Lakshmi-Saraswati, Vishnu, Vinayaka, Bhairao and Aditya. If he is unable to bathe in all the sacred wells, tanks, and bathing ghats on the Ganga, called *tirthas*, he will bathe, at least, in Manikarnika. In that case his pilgrimage will be called *ekatirthi yatra*. If he bathes in Manikarnika, Dasashwamedha, and Panchaganga he will be performing *tritirthi yatra*, but by adding Asi Sangam and Varuna Sangam in his pilgrimage he will be performing *panchatirthi yatra*. Similarly, if he cannot tread on the

Chaurasikroshi or the *panchakroshi-parikrama*, he will circumambulate the main Kashi-kshetra to perform the *antargrihi-parikrama*. The minimum rituals which he performs during his pilgrimage to Kashi are Ganga-pujan, *pitri-sraddha* and *abhiseka* to Visheshwara. If he knows the *mantras* and the methods of sacred performances, he may not employ a priest; but, of course, for certain kinds of rituals, particularly those wherein gifts are to be made, he has to take the help of a Brahmin priest specialized in ritual craft.

It is true that all the Brahmin pilgrims do not fulfil even these minimum requirements of pilgrimage to Kashi, but that is a different question. Here the point of interest is that the Brahmin pilgrim's minimum participation in the pilgrimage is much greater than the ideal requirements of the potter pilgrim. There is another important difference. Unlike the potter, the Brahmin will not visit the shrines of Agiyabir and Lahurabir, nor will he ordinarily bathe in the Krimi-kunda. The potter is the master of his own rituals in the shrines of the deified heroes and the spirits; the Brahmin possesses similar rights in all the Brahminic shrines. In case the latter is illiterate he will employ a priest and even repeat the *mantras*, without understanding their meaning. But in either case he will perform his rituals strictly according to the written text. The potter, on the other hand, follows no text while performing his own rituals. Even while performing the *pindadana* ritual, under the instructions of a Brahmin priest, he is only asked to pronounce the names of his ancestors to whom the *pindas* are to be offered. He might, however, utter a few more vernacular words, as the priest may ask him to do but never the original Vedic text.

Thus, it is obvious that the potter and the Brahmin pilgrims do not participate in the sacred complex in Kashi equally.

The Dandi Sannyasi visiting Kashi may or may not perform any ritual. He may take bath in the Ganga, but not necessarily with a view to wiping out his sins. Also, he may or may not visit any temple. Ideally, he is not expected to perform any textual rituals, as the householders do. As a Vedantin, he is not indeed, supposed to believe in the anthropomorphised forms of gods and goddesses, and hence ideally speaking his visit to a temple is unnecessary. At the time of taking sannyas he had performed the *sraddha* ceremony for his ancestors as well as his own funeral rite which signified his death as "this-worldly" individual. Hence, he is no longer required to follow "this-worldly" laws. His visit to a place of pilgrimage may be casual or motivated by personal needs such as meeting with his fellow-sannyasis, or may be that he is just roving about the places. To him, ideally, there is no distinction between what is socially called 'sacred' and 'profane'.

In practice, however, most Dandi Sannyasis visit temples and perform *abhiseka* to the Panchadevas. But an orthodox Dandi is satisfied only with the worship of his *danda*, the sacred staff. When he passes through a temple he may only touch the temple-gate or even the idol with his *danda*, and go away without performing any *abhiseka*. He may visit the shrine of Augharki Takiya and Keenaramka Astar, and if he is doing *sadhana* he may also sit on the Manikarnika, the cremation ghat. In fact, his behaviour is dependent largely on his personal achievement in *sadhana*. If he is a realized person he will not bother with what is socially called 'sacred' and 'profane', *shastric* and what is *laukic*. But, if he has just dressed himself up in the ochre robe, only to roam about with a *danda*, without understanding his goal, he may behave like an orthodox Brahmin.

Thus, what is significant about the Dandi's visit to Kashi is that his participation in the pilgrimage, in the sense of ritual performances, is practically nil.

ORGANIZATION OF SACRED TRADITIONS

From the foregoing allusions it transpires that the pilgrims belonging to OCT, TCT and TranCT do not participate equally in the sacred complex in Kashi. But, in order to understand such culturally patterned inequality, one must look into the organization of the sacred traditions and the development of the concept of the sacred in each tradition.

Nearly half a century ago, Bose (1929) had suggested a classification of culture according to human desires. Using Hindu scriptural terminology, he divided human desires into three groups, namely, those connected with *artha* or economic needs, *kama* or sexual desires, and *moksha* or the desire for spiritual freedom. A culture is characterized by various *acharas* or institutionalized behaviour which satisfy these impulses through five agencies, namely *vastu* or material object, *kriya* or habitual action, *samhati* or social organization, *viswas mulaka tattwa* or abstract ideas based on faith, and *vichara mulaka tattwa* or the body of knowledge obtained through the application of logical methods. Haldane (1956) had made extensive use of this classification in his Huxley Memorial Lecture while examining the cultural tradition among animals. This may also be fruitfully used in order to explain the organization of the sacred traditions among human beings.

The conception of the sacred is essentially based on man's desire to communicate with the spiritual world, usually in order to attain *moksha*. But, since the desire for *moksha* is conditioned by the desire for emancipation from other desires, the sacred principles are fully reflected in *artha* and *kama* as well. We shall try to examine how the three cultural traditions OCT, TCT and TranCT, have treated the concept of the sacred in satisfying the above desires.

To a peasant potter the entire earth is sacred, and hence, he worships Bhuyian Mata, the Mother Earth. But he considers a place specially sacred when the knowledge of its sacred power is transmitted to him by the oral-experiential method. For instance, a deity appears in dream and discloses her abode, or someone has experienced the manifestation of the sacred power at a particular place, and so the place becomes the centre of worship. It is on account of this sharing of individual experiences that new sacred sites are occasionally discovered in the sacred geography of a region or a village. This can be established by plotting out the places of folk-worship in a region, over time. Such investigation might also show that several old sites have been abandoned and new sacred sites have come up because of the loss of memory or the loss of the "sacred power" in the case of the old sites, and also because of new experiences in favour of the new ones. In OCT, the sacred space is often delimited by such sacred landmarks as hills, rocks, trees, lakes, and rivers. Sometimes, the spread of human or cattle epidemic may also lead to the ritualization of a region or a village. This will indicate the jurisdiction of a malevolent deity responsible for the calamity.

In OCT, the aid of the "sacred power' is sought mainly for the fulfilment of desires related to *artha* and *kama.* For instance, the potter regularly worships Khoriar Devi which protects his earthenwares from dinting at the time of firing. When he makes a pilgrimage to Kashi he pays a special visit to the shrine of Agiyabir which he considers a fire (*agiya*) deity. His prosperity in pottery-making depends largely on the proper firing of the earthenwares, and hence the worship of Agiyabir is important for him. There are several malevolent deities which he worships at the time of performing the fertility rites. When he comes to Kashi he worships Bhuyian Mata and bathes in Krimi-kunda which bestows on him his desired offspring. Thus, he worships the deities which are of immediate help to him in the fulfilment of his economic and reproductive needs. The wrath of the deities may inflict positive harm to his life and living, and hence they are more feared than respected.

In TCT, the concept of the sacred is highly complex, but duly recorded. Since it has evolved through various stages in the development of textual knowledge, over a period of six to seven thousand years, and since all the texts dealing with the subject have been scrupulously and reverentially preserved to this day, one naturally gets lost in the jungle of scriptures. But one's difficulties will be greatly solved if one keeps in mind that the uniqueness of Indian textual tradition lies in producing new texts by interpreting the old ones and linking all the branches of knowledge with one another by maintaining that the Vedas are their ultimate and the common source.

If we look at the origin and development of the *tirthas* we will find that there is a continuity in their sacred tradition. Practically all the *tirthas* are the places where once the Vedic *Rishis* performed *tapas* and created the *mantras*. Since these *Rishis* were the direct seers of Truth and the *mantras* which they created were the embodiment of the sacred, all the places associated with them assumed sacred character. At some of these places, the *Rishis* made gods and goddesses descend and live permanently. Later on, holy men began to visit them frequently, and so they became well-known. With the creation of *Pauranic* literature, detailed descriptions of these places appeared, and some new sacred places were also added to the list, showing the sojourn of gods and goddesses during their earthly incarnations. Each *sampradaya* associated certain places with its tutelary deity, and thus founded its sacred places of pilgrimage. But, at these places the deities of other sects were also subsequently established. The location of the places of pilgrimage, their merits, and the required sacred performances were duly recorded. The holy places were identified and marked by temples, trees, sacred wells, and bathing ghats, and their sacred territories, called *kshetras* and *mandalas*, were also delimited by establishing the tradition of periodical circumambulation.

Thus, in TCT a place or an object becomes sacred by its association with the sacred being. In OCT also the underlying principle may appear to be, more or less, the same, because it holds that the manifestation of the "sacred power" at a place or in an object makes the place and the object sacred. But, the two traditions are fundamentally different in their sources and understanding. In TCT, only those places are externally sacred which have the textual testimony of once being associated with the direct seers of the Truth and/or with the tutelary gods, and where the *devatas* reside. In OCT, on the other hand, all the places are potentially sacred; the sacred may be manifest at any place, at any time, because the entire earth is sacred. From this it also follows that the sanctity of a place will be recognized only until such time as the "sacred power" is manifest and as soon as the situation reverses, the place loses its importance and, hence, abandoned. But, in TCT all the places associated with the direct seers of Truth or gods in their different incarnations have assumed an eternal, sacred character. Since there are now no direct seers of Truth, no new sacred places of eternal value can be founded. A place may still be consecrated by performing certain Vedic rituals, as is usually done at the time of erecting a temple, but it does not acquire the same eternal worth which the original *tirthas* possess, and hence it may be polluted and abandoned. If all the temples in a *tirtha* are polluted or raised to the ground, the sanctity and the efficacy of the *kshetra* shall remain unaffected and hence new temples may still be built at new sites within its sacred territory. This is how the *tirthas* of the Hindus have survived numerous invasions and destructions.

In TCT, ideally, the sacred power is within the creative range of man. The *rishis* have created the *mantras* which are the embodiment of the sacred and the bestower of peace and happiness. Therefore, the sacred is not something which is to be feared. On the other hand, it is to be cultivated and used for the benefit of man. This becomes amply clear if we examine how the sacred is used in TCT.

In TCT, the sacred is used for the fulfilment of all the three cardinal human desires—*artha*, *kama* and *moksha*. This is well-reflected in its organization of gods and goddesses in the concrete forms of the sacred. All the thirtythree hundred million gods and goddesses look after the interest of mankind. Their roles have been specified, and each has been allotted a department concerning a particular kind of human needs. Thus, the goddess Lakshmi takes care of the economic needs of man, the god Kamadeva presides over sexual desire, and the god Shiva liberates man from human sufferings. By invoking these gods and goddesses, human desires are fulfilled, but man is not completely dependent on them. There are sacred *mantras* which have the power to fertilize land, to remove sickness, and to bestow offspring, and to do everything that one may desire.

The sacred has been used in TCT as the vehicle of human feelings and expressions in the form of art and aesthetics, poetry and literature. Even sexual desires have found expressions in temple sculptures, religious dances, dramas, and poetry. They are not only reflected in religious symbolism and literature, but are actualised in the institution of Devadasis, the so-called sacred prostitution. There is no social inhibition on such expressions and performances so long as these are used as a means of communication with the sacred.

The use of the sacred is, however, made not only in the fulfilment of economic and sexual needs, but more conspicuously it is aimed at the final liberation of man which is the end of all desires. Indeed, whenever one invokes a deity he prays for health, wealth and offspring for the enjoyment of worldly pleasure, he also seeks earnestly the *moksha* which is the terminal point of his worldly sufferings.

In TranCT, one begins with the textual conception of the sacred, but as he advances in the pursuit of transcendental knowledge, he discovers the futility of the sacred symbols and performances. At the initial stage, he may make use of the worldly form of the sacred in acquiring the knowledge of the Ultimate Reality. But he does not use the sacred for the fulfilment of economic or sexual needs, for he has already transcended these desires. The manifest form of the sacred is relevant to him only up to a certain stage of his progress in the *sadhana*, and then he gives it up altogether.

INTEGRATION OF DIVERSE TRADITIONS

It may thus be stated that the differences among the pilgrims of the three cultural traditions have arisen mainly from their varied notions and use of the manifest form of the sacred which each of them has inculcated by different modes of learning. But the cultural patterning of their differences in such that they do not fall into conflict. Instead, each of them forms an inseparable part of an organic whole. We shall presently try to explain the philosophical content which serves as a leaven to this unique integration of diverse cultural traditions.

In the sacred complexes of Kashi, the ideal participation of the three cultural traditions may be diagrammatically presented as shown on page 31.

It shows that the TCT. which has created the sacred complex of Kashi, occupies the central position and participates fully in the pilgrimage; the OCT is at the periphery of the Brahamanical sacred complex, and hence minimum participation; while the TranCT goes still farther from the centre, but keeps the OCT within its inner circuit. Since the TranCT is engaged in the pursuit of supreme knowledge, its acceptance of the OCT cannot be challenged by the TCT which pays highest respect to the former. Thus logically, the TCT cannot do without the OCT which forms the medial part of its sacred complex. The philosophical content which holds them together to form the body of a civilization or the religious phenomena is that there are different paths leading to the Truth and one is free to choose a path according to his *svadharma*. Therefore, in the sacred geography of the Brahamanical Kashi, no conflict arises when the people belonging to non-Brahamanical OCT found their own sacred places of worship.

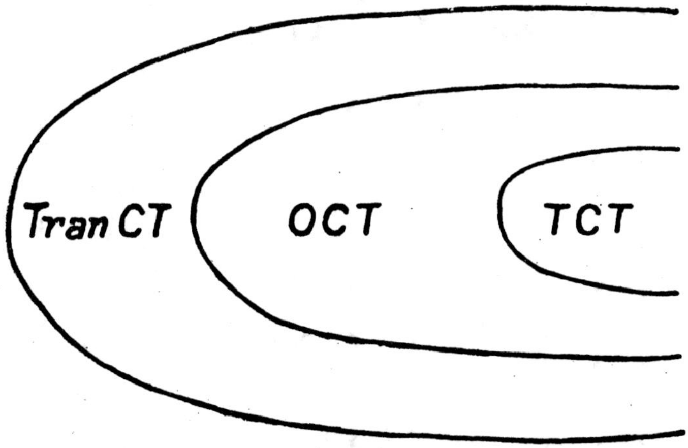

FIG. 1 : *Participation of three cultural traditions in the sacred complexes of Kashi.*

Similar freedom has been granted to all the three traditions to conceptualise the sacred according to their respective system of knowledge. In OCT, the sacred is all-pervading, all-powerful, and is characterized by malevolence, for it causes and removes all kinds of obstacles to the fulfilment of human desires, and hence, it has to be appeased. In TCT, the sacred is usually characterized by benevolence and its power is within the creative range of man. But, to the TranCT the question whether the sacred is malevolent or benevolent is of little importance. For, at a stage where the knower and the known become one and the same, the sacred cannot be distinguished from the one who knows it. Thus, here again, the TranCT levels down the differences between TCT and OCT on their notions of the sacred, treating both the notions negatively.

At the ideal level, the sacred is largely used by the OCT for the fulfilment of *artha* and *kama* needs; in TCT it is used for the fulfilment of all the three cardinal human desires—*artha*, *kama*, and *moksha:* but the TranCT makes use of it only in the pursuit of *moksha*. The concept of *moksha* is indigenously absent in OCT. But when the people belonging to this tradition make a pilgrimage to Kashi they invoke Visheshwara and the Ganga who, according to the TCT, are the liberators of mankind. This, of course, they do without understanding the philosophy of liberation. In borrowing the concept of *moksha* from the TCT they are obviously motivated by their desire to be free from worldly sufferings and to be duly rewarded in the next birth of which they have only a vague notion.

The Hindu concept of *moksha* is the product of the TranCT, but it finds its textual expressions in TCT. It holds that men, animals, insects, birds, reptiles, plants and trees, and all other things which have life have also the soul and in the cycle of birth and death their positions are interchangeable, and it is the soul which is liberated and not the man or the animal. All the souls are the particles of the Supreme Soul, *Paramatma*. They are lost in the worldly *maya* (illusion) and hence separated from the *Purusa*. But their ultimate goal is to unite with the *Purusa*. This conception of soul as a universal principle, present in all living beings provides Hinduism with a unique position in the field of religion. For, the other religions have reserved the 'kingdom of god' for the mankind alone; in some religions it is only for a selected few.

The concept of soul makes one realize that all living beings on the earth are the manifestations of the *Paramatma* and hence basically sacred. From the concept that the whole Truth is incommunicable and one can express only the partial Truth, it arises that our knowledge of the sacred is after all only partial, and, therefore, we cannot legitimately question the veracity of the concept which is contrary to our views. In view of this, there is no scope in Hinduism to hold something 'sacred' as opposed to something which might be called 'profane'. This questions the Durkheimian theory (1964: 37) that all known religious beliefs presuppose a classification of all the things, real and ideal, of which men think, into two classes or opposed groups, generally designated by two distinct terms, *profane* and *sacred*.

The Hindu philosophical interpretation of the sacred has influenced social realities to such an extent that in the sacred

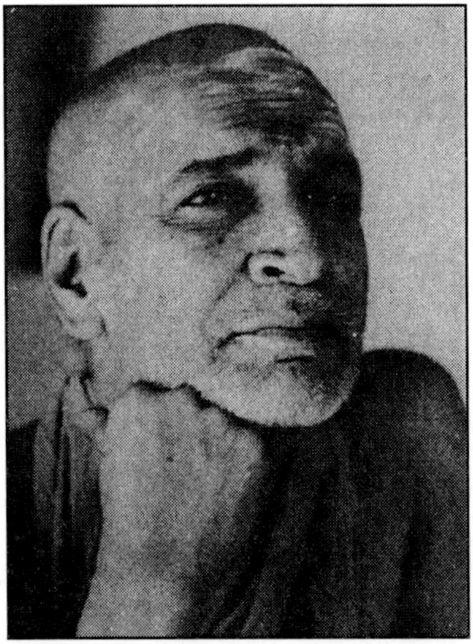

1. Swami Karpatrijee – a sacred intellectual

2. A Dandi *sannyasi* at worship

3. Mother Annapurna of Varanasi

4. A South Indian deity taken round in procession in a palanquin

complex of Kashi, even at the behavioural level, it is difficult to make out a clear distinction between the sacred and the secular, or the sacred and the profane. For instance, the professional behaviour of the Brahmin priests who officiate in a temple or conduct rituals at the ghat is not at all different from those who are engaged in secular occupations like carpentry or fishmongering. Their argument is that they cultivate 'sacred' for their livelihood or *vritti*. Therefore, when they bargain with the pilgrims or even adopt nefarious means to extract money from them they are doing nothing more than what the fishmongers do in their *vritti*. Similarly, the sacred-profane dichotomy remains no longer a social reality when the Doms of Kashi are made the custodians of the sacred fire. These Doms of the OCT, in another context, fall into the category of untouchables. But the people belonging to the TCT, including the orthodox Brahmins, can get *moksha* only when their bodies have been cremated by the sacred fire procured from the Doms. Although the people belonging to the TranCT have no such necessity of procuring the sacred fire from the Doms (for most of them are not cremated but immersed or buried) yet when they reach to the stage of *turiyatita* they clearly show in their behaviour no distinction between what others might call 'sacred' and 'profane'.

Thus, it may be concluded that although the sacred complex in Kashi may appear predominantly Brahminic, it is indeed a much bigger organization of sacred tradition, which makes the Brahminical temple of Visheshwar and the non-Brahminical shrine of Agiyabir co-exist, the textually learned *Karmakandis* and the illiterate untouchable Doms to conduct the sacred performances together, and a *naisthika* Brahmin touch the feet of an *avadhoota* who eats carcasses. This kind of arrangement in sacred places of pilgrimage demonstrates and reminds the pilgrims coming from different cultural traditions, again and again, that they must not be too egoistic in upholding their own tradition as the superiormost. For, their differences in the conception and treatment of the sacred—the highest *achara*—have arisen mainly from the varied modes of acquisition and transmission of knowledge. Each of them, in accordance with their respective traditions, gives different weightage to the fulfilment of the three cardinal human desires, but all the differences melt away in their desire for *moksha*, which is the end of all desires and which leads all the living beings together to unite with the ultimate. It really does not matter what path one adopts in the pursuit of *moksha* so long as it reaches the same goal.

If this lesson of pilgrimage is brought home, there is no reason why one cannot live and work together with the people of varied cultural traditions without getting engulfed in communal or sectarian tension.

REFERENCES

Bose, Nirmal Kumar, 1929. *Cultural Anthropology*, Calcutta.

Cohn, Bernard S. and McKim Marriott, 1958. Networks and centres in the integration of Indian civilization, *Journal of Social Research* (1).

Durkheiam, Emile, 1964. *The Elementary Forms of the Religious Life*, London.

Haldane, J.B.S., 1956. The argument from animals to men: an examination of its validity for anthropology, *The Journal of the Royal Anthropological Institute of Great Britain and Ireland*, 86(II).

Saraswati, Baidyanath, 1970. *Contribution to the Understanding of Indian Civilization*, Dharwar.

Vidyarthi, L.P., 1961. *The Sacred Complex in Hindu Gaya*, Bombay.

3

THE SACRED JOURNEY
Traditions of Pilgrimage in India

THE CONCEPT of the sacred complex ranges across widely diverse dimensions. One of the dimensions which I have suggested elsewhere[1] displays the resilience of secular institutions running along the sacerdotal system. Much of it has been obtained from the "self-view" of the "insiders" of a *tirtha*—the people living there as citizens, not pilgrims. What emerged in this study was unconventional but refreshing. In conclusion, it was noted that, unlike the Semitic cultures, in the Indian tradition the sacred is in tune with the secular and hence we cannot possibly draw an exclusive model of the sacred complex to which the secular would be peripheral.

Another dimension of the sacred complex, which awaits examination and which indeed is of prime importance, relates itself to a synchronic-diachronic view of the organization of its traditions. From what I have seen of the major *tirthas* it is almost obvious to me that various regions of India have organized their traditions of the sacred complex variously. The study of Kashi has already shown that it creates and accommodates varieties of sacred traditions. But if this is so, then what is the basis for the relationship between one tradition and another? How could the unity of civilization comes about through pilgrimage—the sacred journey? And, why was the diversity of traditions allowed to perpetrate? These are some of the basic questions which must be examined closely to achieve such understanding of the traditions of *tirthas* as is still lacking in anthropological literature. To begin with, let us seek to answer the foremost question: How did the textual authorities conceive the form of a *tirtha*?

CONCEPTUAL CATEGORIES

Tirtha

The Vedic word *tirtha*[2] (Pali, Prakrita—*tittha*), from *ter*, *tarate*, means ford, steps to a river, place of pilgrimage. In course of time its meaning and scope were extended to all things held to be pure and holy. *Tirthas* exist in various forms, namely, speech, water, land, body, limbs, time, trees, places resorted to by gods, places where there are images of gods, and so on. The feet of a Brahmin, the back of a cow, the limb of one's own wife, one's own eyes and the right ear are *tirthas.*[3] The part at the little finger of a twice-born man is called the *tirtha* sacred to Prajapati; the part at the root of the thumb is called *tirtha* sacred to Brahmin; the part at the tops of the fingers is called the *tirtha* sacred to gods; and the part of the root of the forefinger is called the *tirtha* sacred to the manes.[4] One finds mention of *kala-tirthas*[5] (that is, *tirthas* in the form of auspicious time) which are said to be Vaishnava, Shakta, and Shaiva. The days and occasions regarded as *kala-tirthas* are Varah-dvadashi in Margasirsha-shukla-paksha, Ananta-chaturdasi in Bhadra-shukla-paksha, the day for worship of Karttikeya in the month of Kartika, the time for the study of the *Puranas* and so on. Months have been classified into *Saura* (solar) and *Chandra* (lunar); of these, Asadha, Kartika, Magh, and Vaisakha are *tirthas.*[6] Places where *agnihotra* and *sraddha* are performed, a temple, a house where the Veda is being studied, a cowpen, the place where a *soma* drinker dwells, parks, a place where the *asvastha* exists, a place where the *Purana* is being recited or where one's teacher stands or where a chaste housewife dwells or where a father and a worthy son dwell are *tirthas.*[7] Sanctity is caused to a place by the presence of lotus-plants, *tulasi* (basil) plants, and *bilva* (wood-apple) trees.[8] Water has been considered as a potent agent in the removal of sin. Holy or consecrated water is *tirtha*. Particular sanctity has been attached to river-fords, certain divine waters, also mountains and forests.

Tirthas are held to be holy, on three grounds, namely, on account of some wonderful natural characteristic of the locality, on account of the peculiar strikingness (or grandeur) of some watery place, or on account of the fact that some (holy) sages resorted to them (for bathing, austerities, and so on). *Tirtha*, therefore, means a locality or spot or expanse of water which gives rise to the accumulation of righteousness (merit) owing to its own peculiar nature without any adventitious circumstance[9] (such as the presence of *salagrama* near it). Its antiquity is evidenced by literature of Brahmanism, Buddhism and Jainism.

In the Rig Veda,[10] waters, rivers in general and certain rivers mentioned by name are referred to with great reverence as divine and are deified. In the hymns of the Atharva Veda[11] waters are described as holy and purifying, and invoked to heal various kinds of diseases and to confer happiness and prosperity. The confluence of rivers and the valleys of mountains have been described in the Vedas as especially holy. The sanctity of the rivers and mountains has been stressed in the *Smritis*, the *Dharmasutras* and the *Puranas*. In these scriptures, particularly in the *Puranas* pilgrimage to holy places, holy mountains, and holy rivers has been highly lauded as the remover of sins (*pap*) and bestower of merits (*punya*). Some of the *Puranas* such as *Skanda*, *Padma* and *Narada*, however, emphasize one's personal purity and virtue as essential qualifications[12] for obtaining the full merit of pilgrimage. It is in this context that truth, compassion and self-restraint have been called *manas-tirthas*. Similarly, Brahmans (the virtuous ones) are said to be *jangam* (mobile) *tirtha*: places of pilgrimage are *sthavar tirthas*, parents, preceptors, husbands and wife are also *tirtha*.

The *Mahaparinibbana Suttanta* mentions the four holy places of the Buddhists, namely, Lumbini, Gaya, Sarnath and Kushinagar. Places such as Rajgriha, Vaishali, Mankul Parvata, Sunsmargiri, Parileyak, Nala and Vairanjja where the Buddha used to spend the rainy season (*varsavasa*) every year have been described as holy. The places where he performed miracles are also considered holy, such Sankasya where he is believed to have descended from heaven. Vaishali where monkeys offered him honey, Rajgriha where he subdued a mad elephant, and Sravasti where he performed the miracle of reduplicating himself. The eight original places where the relics of the Buddha were kept and the *stupas* erected thereon became especially holy for the Buddhists. Buddhists from all over the world visit these holy places periodically with a view to acquiring merits.

In Jain scriptures, the *jin shasana* (*dharma*) is itself the 'real' *tirtha*. The one who creates *tirtha* is Tirthankara. The places associated with the conception, birth, contemplation, *kaivalya* and *nirvana* of all the twenty-four Tirthankaras are holy for the Jains. These *tirthas* are spread all over India. They have been divided into two classes—*siddha-kshetra* and *atisaya-kshetra*. The places where the Tirthankaras and other holy men have attained *nirvana* are *siddha-kshetra*; those which have assumed importance because of temples, idols, or certain miraculous events are the *atisaya-kshetra*.

Thus, in all the major cultural traditions of India the concept of *tirtha* as 'sacred' has appeared prominently. While some scriptures have laid too much stress on pilgrimage to sacred spots as the most effective means of expiation for all sins, others have laid importance on the righteous way of life in addition to it. But, in either case the importance of a sacred spot, because of its association with either gods or saints or founders of faith has been recognized.

There are countless *tirthas*. The list[13] given in all the major *Puranas* and the *Mahabharata* is very large and yet incomplete. According to the *Brahma Purana*[14] their number is so large that they cannot be enumerated in detail even in hundreds of years. The *Matsya Purana*[15] (110.7) declares that there are 35 millions of *tirthas* in *divi* (sky) in *antariksha* (the aerial regions) and on *bhumi* (the earth) and all of them are located in the Ganga; the *Vamana Purana* gives this figure for the *lingas* alone. The *Sabdakalpadruma* which has utilised this form of literature more than any other indigenous work of reference presents a more realistic picture of the *tirthas* by arranging 264 of them in the order of their due circumambulation from the left to the right.

Many *tirthas* are named in one place. It is believed that

thirtythree crores of *tirthas* are located in Kashi but in actual enumeration none of the *Puranas* has mentioned more than three hundred names. Similarly, the *Mahabharata* (*Vanaparva* 82.21) remarks that all the ten crores of *tirthas* are present in Pushkar—this obviously does not indicate their actual number. The 200 *yojana* long Godavari is also believed to have three crores and a half of *tirthas* in it. Thus, in a major *tirtha* are enshrined several important and cognate *tirthas* which may be called its *upa-tirthas*.

The *Brahma Purana* (70.16-9) classifies *tirthas* into four divisions, namely, *daiva* (created by gods), *asura* (those associated with *asuras*), *arsa* (those established by sages), and *manus* (created by kings like Ambarisa, Manu and Kuru). Kashi, Pushkara and Prabhasa are sanctified by all the three gods. The Sarasvati springs from Brahma, the Ganga from Vishnu, and the Narmada from Shiva. Among *tirthas* called *daiva* are the Ganga, the Yamuna, the Sarasvati, the Jhelam, the Beas, the Godavari, the Bhima, the Tungabhadra, the Krisna-veni, the Tapti and the Pain-Ganga. Reservoirs which are not due to human labour are called *daivakhata* (dug by god). Gaya is an *asura tirtha*. Naranarayana is an *arsa tirtha*. These classes of *tirthas* are assigned to the Krta, Treta, Dvapara, and Kali *yugas*.

Most of the writers of digests (*nibandhas* and *mahtmya granthas*) on *tirthas* have described some *tirthas* as more meritorious than others.[16] The *Tirthakalpataru* of Lakshmidhar, one of the earliest digests (about A.D. 1110-1120), and the *Trishathalisetu* of Narayanabhatta attach the highest importance to Kashi. The *Tirthasara* deals with *tirthas* in the Deccan and South India and lauds the *mahatmya* of Setubandha, Pundarika (Pandharpur), Godavari, Krisna-venya, and Narmada. The *Puranas* and the *Mahabharata* have placed various *tirthas* in a hierarchy of merits. Thus, Naimisa is the best *tirtha* on the earth and Puskar in the aerial region, while Kurukshetra is the most distinguished in all the three worlds (*Vanaparva*, 82.20). Kurukshetra is holy, Sarasvati is holier than Kurukshetra, and Prithudaka is the holiest of all *tirthas* (*Vanaparva*, 83.145). The water of the Sarasvati purifies after one bathes for three days, those of the Yamuna in seven days, those of the Ganga at once, while the water of the Narmada purifies a man at the mere sight of it (*Matsya Purana*, 186.11). There is no place higher than Varanasi, nor will there be one (*Kurma Purana*, I. 31.64). The reward that is secured by pilgrimage to Varanasi, Kurukshetra, and Narmada can be secured at Dwarka in half a twinkle (*Skanda Purana* 44.4.52). Prayaga is the king of all *tirthas* and hence the epithet "Prayagaraja".

Four of the most important and holy *tirthas* are located in four corners of the country, namely, Badrinath in the north, Puri in the east, Rameshvaram in the south, and Dwarka in the west. These are styled *dhama*. Similarly, there is a group of seven sacred cities (*sapta puri*) believed to be the bestower of *moksha*. They are Ayodhya, Mathura, Maya (Haridvara), Kashi, Kanchi (or Kanti), Avantika (Ujjain) and Dwarka. There are twelve *Jyotirlingas* of Shiva which receive the highest veneration. They are Somanath in Saurashtra, Malikarjuna on Srisaila hill in the Kurnool district, Mahakal in Ujjain, Parmesvara in Omkara-kshetra in the Narmada, Kedar in the Himalayas, Bhimshankar in Dakini at the source of the Bhima river near Poona, Visheshvara in Kashi, Trayambakesvara on the bank of the Gautami (Godavari) near Nasik, Vaidyanath in Chitabhumi, Nagesa in Darukavana, Rameshvara in Setubandha and Ghrishnesa in Shivalaya at the famous site of Elura.

All rivers falling into the sea, all seas, and all great mountains and forests have been declared holy, but some of them are especially holy. There are seven seas (Sindhu's), seven forests, and seven mountains (Kulaparvata/s) of great merit. The confluence of rivers and springs makes a place especially holy. The "Triveni" at Prayaga, where the rivers Ganga, Yamuna and Sarasvati meet together, is endowed with special merit. The Sapta-pushkarni at Thid in Kashmir is holy because seven springs unite there. Saptarishikunda becomes important because seven *dharas* (fountain) fall there from Himavata.

There are fiftyfive sacred places which are fittest for *sraddha* performances. Of these again, Gaya is the most important for sacrifice.

Some *tirthas* have acquired such great importance that others are named after them. There are five Prayagas in the Himalayas, each at the confluence of two rivers:

(1) Devaprayaga (confluence of Bhagirathi and Alaknanda), (2) Karnaprayaga (Alaknanda and Pindara), (3) Rudraprayaga (Alaknanda and Mandakini), (4) Nandaprayaga (Alaknanda and Nanda), and (5) Visnuprayaga (Alaknanda and Visnuganga). They are collectively referred to as Pancha-Prayaga. Similarly, there are five rivers each called Ganga, namely Bhagirathi, Godavari, Krishna, Pinakini (Pennar) and Kaveri. These are known as Pancha-Ganga.

As in the case of rivers, so in the case of *tirthas* there lies the importance of *pancha-tirtha.* In Kashi the five essential *tirthas* are Dashashvamedha, Lolarka, Keshava, Bindumadhava, and Manikarnika. The *Kashi Khanda* of the *Skanda Purana* gives another list of the five *tirthas* called *pancha-tirtha,* which every pilgrim to Kashi must visit, namely, the confluence of the Asi with the Ganga, Dashashavamedha, Manikarnika, Panchaganga and the confluence of the river Varna (Varuna) with the Ganga. In Puri, the *pancha-tirthas* are the pool of Markandeya, the *vata* tree (identified with Krishna), Balarama, the sea, and the Indradyumna pool.

There are five Kedara/s, namely, Kedarnatha, Tunganatha, Rudranatha, Madhyamesvara, and Kalpesvara. Also there are five Badri, namely, Vishala-Badri (in Badrinath), Yogadhyana-Badri (in Pandukesavara), Bhavishya-Badri (in Sujnanien), Vriddha-Badri (in Anni *matha*) and Dhyana-Badri (in Urghava). There are five holy *shilas* in Badrinath-Kshetra, namely, Garuda-shila, Narada-shila, Markandya-shila, Narsingh-shila, Varahi-shila and Kapal-mochana.

Similarly, there are seven Gangas and seven Godavaris. The rivers included in the list of Sapta-Ganga are Ganga, Godavari, Kaveri, Tamraparni, Sindhu, Saryu and Narmada. The Sapta-Godavari refers to the seven mouths of the Godavari sacred to seven sages, namely, Kasyapa, Atri, Gautama, Bharadvaja, Vishvamitra, Jamadagni and Vashitha. The Godavari falls into the sea with seven mouths, and hence is very sacred.

To conclude: (a) although it may not be possible to place all the *tirthas* into a commonly acceptable hierarchical order, the fact that they are of unequal merits and importance cannot be denied; (b) the grading of *tirthas* takes into account the holy places from each region of India; and (c) certain most important holy places are represented by their counterparts in different regions.

Kshetra

In the *Pauranic* description of sacred spots one comes across the concept of *kshetra*. Literally, the word *kshetra*[17] means landed property, field, an enclosed spot of ground, portion or space, place or origin, superficies, circuit, region, seat, sphere of activity, source, extent, womb, wife, seat of the soul, body (regarded as the field of the working of the soul), primeval soul or matter, a house, a town, a plane-figure as a triangle. By prefixing it to terms of religious significance its primary meaning has been extended in scriptures to a number of well-developed concepts such as *kshetra-adhidevata*: the tutelary deity of any sacred piece of ground, *kshetra-devata*: the deity of the field, *kshetra-padam:* a place sacred to a deity, *kshetra-pal*: a deity protecting fields—an epithet of Shiva, *kshetra-vida*: a sage—one who has spiritual knowledge, *kshetraja*: a fifteen year old girl personating Durga at a festival, *kshetrastha:* residing at a sacred place, *kshetra-sannyas*: living in retirement at a sacred place under a vow not to transcend its geographic boundary under any circumstance.

The concept of *buddha-kshetra*[18] (Pali, *khetta*) occurs in several of the Buddhist scriptures. It means Buddha field, region or (usually) world or world system in which a particular Buddha lives and operates. The 'jewels' of *buddha-kshetra* are Bodhisattavas. There is also the concept of *buddhasunya buddha-kshetram* which implies that the Buddhas are not produced in all Buddha-fields and hence in many there is no Buddha at all. The *buddha-kshetra* has been equated with *lokadhatu*, meaning merely world system, presumably as potential field for a Buddha, but not necessarily containing one. The *upa-kshetra*, subordinate (Buddha) field, has been stated to be four times the size of a (Buddha) *kshetra*; the implication seems to be that the environs of the *kshetra* constitute the *upa-kshetra*.

According to the *Hevajra Tantra*,[19] the *kshetras* are Munmuni, Karunyapataka, Devikota and Karmarapataka; the *upa-kshetras* are Kulata, Arbuda, Godavari and Himadri.

All *tirthas* are not *kshetra*. In the Brahmanic scriptures some of the *tirthas* are described as *siddha-kshetra*, the place of supreme attainments. Such are Varanasi-kshetra (also known as Kashi-kshetra, and Avimuktaka-kshetra, because it is free from *avi*-sin, and is never forsaken by Shiva), Kamrup-kshetra, Bhaskara-kshetra or Arka-kshetra, Purshottama-kshetra or Sri-kshetra, Ganga-kshetra, Narayana-kshetra, Gaya-kshetra, and Prayag-kshetra or Prajapati-kshetra. As embodiments of gods and goddesses these are *mukti-kshetra*—places of salvation. Among other *kshetras* are mentioned Ahi-kshetra, Bhrigu-kshetra, Brahma-kshetra, Dharma-kshetra (same as Kurukshetra), Druma-kshetra, Gaja-kshetra, Harihar-kshetra, Haya-kshetra, Kedara-kshetra, Nandi-kshetra, Pundarika-kshetra, Sureshvari-kshetra, Varahamula-kshetra or Varah-kshetra, Vastrapatha-kshetra or Ravataka-kshetra, etc. These are *punya-kshetras*—holy places.

All the *kshetras* being the sacred dwellings of the deities included in the four principal Hindu pantheon, these are placed under a four-fold broad classification: Brahma-kshetra, Vishnu-kshetra, Shiva-kshetra and Shakti-kshetra. For example: Kuru-kshetra is Brahma-kshetra, Puri is Vishnu-kshetra, Bhuvaneshwar is Shiva-kshetra, and Jaipur is Parvati-kshetra. According to the *Narsingh Purana*[20] there are sixty-eight Vishnu-kshetras, each giving a different epithet to Vishnu. Similarly, there are other gods and goddesses associated with *kshetras*: Kumbhakonam is Ganapati-kshetra,[21] called Svetavighneswara-kshetra; Konaraka is Surya-kshetra; Narmada is Bhrugu-kshetra; in Kashmir Baramula is Varaha-kshetra; also Nandi-kshetra and Gaja-kshetra. Some of the *kshetras* are shared by more gods than one of equal importance. Kashi is well-known as a Shiva-kshetra, it is also a Vishnu-kshetra, because here Vishnu assumes the epithet of Keshava; Prayaga is Prajapati-kshetra, also Vishnu-kshetra; and Kanchi is both Vaishnava and Shakta-kshetra.

Identification of a *kshetra*[22] is at times much against the grain, particularly because of the inadequacy of information on ancient geography of India. Many *kshetras* which find mention in the *Puranas* have not yet been located. Sometimes two places claim the same *kshetra* identity. A place called Devata on Tungabhadra, on the boundary between Mysore and Maharashtra, is called Harihar-kshetra; the junction of the Gandaki with the Ganga at Sonpur where *Gajendra-moksha* took place is also known as Harihar-kshetra. Ahi-kshetra as a place associated with Drona has been identified by some scholars as one in north Panchala or Rohilkhanda (districts of Budaon and Farukhabad in western Uttar Pradesh); others located it near the Vindhyas or the Narmada. According to one text Konaraka is Bhasakara-kshetra, another describes Prayaga as the Bhaskara-kshetra.

Mandala

Larger than *kshetra* is the sacred territory called *mandala* such as Braja-mandala, Okha-mandala, Saraswata-mandala, Kashmira-mandala, Mahisa-mandala, Prayaga-mandala and Viraja-mandala which extends beyond Jaipur on the river Vaitarni in Orissa. The Tantric Buddhist literature describes the ordering of the *mandala*[23] by means of which a pupil is consecrated. But here *mandala* is inscribed in a spot or in a house as *Tantric* drawings of small size (generally three cubics plus three inches), using the sacred writing colours or powder made from the five gems, or the grains of rice and so on.

Pitha

The term *pitha* has especially been used for some places of pilgrimage, generally associated with the Shakta deities. There are Shakta-*pithas*, variously described as 51, 52, 72 or 108 in number each possessing a mutilated limb of Sati, the consort of Shiva. Among them the most important is Kamakhya. The four cardinal centres of ascetic organization which the Adya Shankaracharya had established in four corners of India, namely, Puri in the east, Joshimatha in the north, Dwarka in the west and Sringeri in the south, are also called *pithas*.

In Tantrik Buddhism[24] the terms *pitha* and *upa-pitha* have been used. The *pithas* are Jalandhara, Oddiyana, Purangiri and Kamrupa, the *upa-pithas* are Malava, Sindhu and Nagara. Among the terms for other kinds of sacred territory, which find mention there, are *chandoha* and *pilava*. The *chandohas* are Harikela, arising in the salt ocean, Lampaka, Kanchika, and Saurashtra; the *upa-chandohas* are Kalinga, the Isle of Gold, and Konkana. The *pilavas* comprise that which lies on the village boundary, and that belongs to the city; Caritra, Kosala, Vindhyakumara-purika. The *upa-pilava* is nearby to that.

According to the Buddhist Tantra, the names of the places called *kshetra pithas* and so on, are mentioned for the benefit of simple fools who wander about the country. They are, therefore, interpreted as symbols for the places within the body that is to say that they are the external equivalent of that which exists within.[25] The beautiful verse underlying this theme reads as follows:[26]

When the mind goes to rest,
The bonds of the body are destroyed,
And when the one flavour of the Innate pours forth,
There is neither outcaste nor brahmin.
Here is the sacred Jamuna and here the river Ganges,
Here are Prayaga and Benaras, here are Sun and Moon.
Here I have visited in my wanderings.
    shrines and such places of pilgrimage,
For I have not seen another shrine blissful
    like my own body.

In conclusion, it might be said that the concept of *tirtha* seems to be older than that of the *kshetra.* Possibly the concept of *kshetra* was introduced by the Buddhists in the context of *Tantrika* symbolism, later it was used by the writers of the *Puranas* in planning the sacred territory of a *Tirtha* without changing its significance and symbolic structure. Textual evidence may subsequently be sought to modify this contextual speculation.

STRUCTURE AND ORGANIZATION

Physiognomy of tirthas

Perhaps there is hardly any beauty spot—a spot with natural scenery, a mountain peak, a river, a streamlet, reservoir of water or waterfall which is not marked as *tirtha.* The snow-clad mountain peaks such as Kailash and Nanda Devi, the source of a river such as Gangotri and Yamunotri, the confluence of rivers as in Prayaga and of three oceans as in Kanyakumari, and the reservoirs of holy waters such as Pushkara and Martanda are well-known *tirthas*. The hot-spring (*tapa-kunda*) is called *agni-tirtha*. The eternal flame of the natural gas at Jwalamukhi, the snow *linga* of Shiva at Amarnath, and the sea islands of Rameshwaram and Beta-Dwarka are the examples of natural *tirthas*.

Sacred trees such as *vata*, *pipal*, *kadamba*, *tulsi*, *bilva* and mango are at places worshipped as *upa-tirthas*. Akshya-vata (the imperishable *vata*) also called Kalpadruma is *upa-tirtha* under Prayaga, Puri, Gaya, Godavari and Narmada. Gridhra-vata is *upa-tirtha* under Gaya, and Siddhavata under Ujjain. There is also Kushi-vata *tirtha*. In Gujarat, near Bharucha, the holy place of the Kabirpanthis, is the Kabir-vata. The goddess Meenakshi at Madurai is called Kadamba-vana-vasini, residing in the forest of Kadamba trees. The Kadamba-vana was also a favourite sporting ground of Krishna. The shrine of Ekamranath in Kanchi is the place where Shiva is believed to have appeared before Gauri under the mango tree, and hence the mango tree is sacred. Among the forests marked as *tirthas* are Naimisaranya, Vrindavana, Danda-karanya, Devadaruvana, the twelve *vanas* in Mathura, and the seven holy forests in Kurukshetra, namely, Kamyaka, Aditi-vana, Vyasavana, Phalakivana, Suryavana, Madhuvana and Punyasitavana.

Throughout India places associated with gods, goddesses and saints are converted into temple towns and sacred cities. In South India, temples are characterized by their massive and magnificent structure, imposing *gopuras*, and concentric walled enclosures. In some *tirtha-nagaras*, besides the temples there may be natural spots such as sacred wells and tanks, lakes, and bathing *ghats* all marked as the removers of sins and hence treated as the *upa-tirtha*.

There are also cave temples such as Amarnath in Kashmir, Seeta-gupha in Chitrakoot and the famous Elura cave.

Anthropomorphization of tirthas

As stated, Prayaga is the king of *tirthas*. The *saptapuri* are the *pataranis* (queens) of Prayagaraja. All *tirthas* propitiate him. One of the popular myths about Prayagaraja runs as follows: On the occasion of the *kumbha mela* the bathers leave their sins at the sacred *sangam* (the confluence of rivers) and hence the white colour of the horse of Prayagaraja turns into black. But then the *Tirtharaja* goes to Ayodhya, bathes there in the river Saryu to wash away the black sins, and finally returns to his place galloping on the white horse. According to the *Vanaparva* (85.75) the country between the Ganga and the Yamuna is the hips and loins of the mother earth, and Prayaga is the inmost part of the hips Similarly, Mathura is the horn of the earth, the hump of Madhyadesa.

The sacred rivers like Ganga, Yamuna, Godavari, Narmada, Krishna and Kaveri, in fact all rivers, excepting the Brahmaputra (the son of Brahma), are females. The sacred hills and oceans are males. The Ganga is the mother of all living beings, the Narmada the daughter of the *pitris*. All the holy places in the three worlds come for a bath to the Narmada. Being females all the rivers go through the periods of impurity (*rajodosa*) for three days. The Ganga is however, always pure. Under Gaya-kshetra there is a *upa-tirtha* called *yoni-dwara*—the vaginal passage.

The lay-out of the tirtha

The sacred territory of most *tirthas* is well-planned. The *Pauranic* description in respect of, at least, some of the *kshetras* is complete and graphic, giving such details as total area, location of shrines and boundaries. Here are a few examples:

The Prayaga-mandala is five *yojanas* in circumference and the moment a man enters inside this strip of land, there is an *ashvamedha* at every step (*Matsya Purana*, 108.9-10, 111.8; *Padma Purana*, I.45.8). Prayaga extends from Pratisthana up to the pool of Vasuki and up to the two *nagas* Kambala and Ashvatara and the *naga* Bahumulaka (*Matsya Purana*, 104.5). Veni or Triveni is within Prayaga, twenty bow-lengths (one bow=4 *hastas* 96 *angulas*) in extent.

The Kashi-kshetra is of two *yojanas* and a half east and west and half a *yojana* broad north and south, out of this Varanasi extends up to the river Asi (*Matsya Purana*, 184.50-2). The *Padma Purana* describes the tract covered by a circle, the radius of which is the line joining *Madhyameshvara linga* with the shrine of Dehali Vinayaka. The *Linga Purana* (92.99-100) makes it a *kshetra* of four *kroshas* in extent in the four directions and also one *yojana*. The *Naradiya Purana* (48.18-9) says that the *kshetra* extends over two *yojanas* and a half from east to west and is half a *yojana* wide from north to south; god Sambhu declared the extent of the *kshetra* between the rivers Varuna and Asi. In the *Padma Purana* (14.194-6), Brahma is mentioned to have said to Rudra, I have given you a *kshetra* extending to five *kroshas*; when the best of rivers, Ganga, will flow through this *kshetra*, the city will be great and holy; the Ganga as it flows northwards for two *yojanas* will be holy. According to Pali texts,[27] Avimukta (Kashi) is that part of the holy place which is represented by a radius of 200 *dhanus* (about 1200 feet) in all four directions from the shrine of Visheshwara. Thus the texts differ on the extent of the Kashi-kshetra, but there is a general agreement that Varanasi is that strip of land, the four boundaries of which are the Ganga to the east, Asi to the South, the shrine of Dehali Vinayaka to the west and the river Varuna to the north. According to the *Puranas* the physical appearance of Kashi has been changing. In the Krtya it looked like a trident, in the Treta it assumed circular form, in the Dwapara it took the form of a chariot, and in the Kali *yuga* it has a conch-like shape. The *Skanda Purana* devotes one full chapter to Kashi (*Kashi-Khanda*), giving a detailed plan of the *kshetra*. The Kashi-kshetra is divided into three segments (*khandas*) called Visheshwara-khanda, Kedar-khanda, and Omkara-khanda, each having a presiding god. The text describes at great length the location of the various shrines which the pilgrims are enjoined to worship and circumambulate. The circumambulation of the inner circuits along the three *khandas* is known as *antargrihi parikrama*. Another circuit which goes round in the radius of five *krosha* (16 km) marks the boundary of Kashi-kshetra. The circumambulation on this circuit is known as *panchakroshi parikrama*.

Such description of the area, location and circumambulation of the shrines can be obtained also in respect of Naimisarnya, Gaya, Kurukshetra, and many other *tirthas*.

5. Pilgrims bathing at the Hardwar *Kumbha*

6. Performing the ritual of *Tuladan* (gifting of gold and goods of the weight of the donor)

Organization of the sacred space

The organization of the sacred space or the temple complex in South India[28] is as follows: The most sacred spot is the *pitha* or the pedestal for the idol. The *pitha* is enshrined in a circular or rectangular or sometimes square shaped *sanctum sanctorum* called *garbha-griha*. The roof of the *garbha-griha* is conical or pyramidal (*shikhara*), crowned by a creat (*stupika*). The *garbha-griha* is encircled by the first *prakara* called *antaramandala*. Small *balipithas* representing the eight *dikapalas* and the seven *matris* etc. are placed here. A flight of steps called *sopana* connects this *prakara* with the door of the *garbha-griha*. In front of the *sopana* is the main *mandapa*. Round this *mandapa* and *antaramandala* is the second *prakara* called *antahara*, forming a broad verandah with doorways on all the four sides. The *antahara* leads out into an enclosure containing the main *balipith*. After the *antahara* we get the third *prakara* called *madhyahara* which is essentially a continuous structure having an array of lamps all round from top to bottom. Beyond this and just outside the main *balipitha* is the flagstaff (*dhvajastambha*). The fourth *prakara* called *bahyahara* is beyond this. It forms the pathway for the processions within the temple. The fifth and last *prakara* is the outermost wall of the temple. This is called *maryada*. The main entrance is through a *gopura* which may be an ordinary door way with small roofing or one with a superstructure comprising rooms and verandah. The space between the *garbha-griha* and *antahara* is roofless; so also is most of the space between the *madhyahara* and *maryada*.

Thus the comparative holiness of space in South India temple complex terminates at the outermost wall called *maryada* (limit).

In the North Indian *Pauranic* organization of sacred space there is no such artificial limit. The holiest spot is the *garbha-griha*, and then in the descending order are the *prakara*, the *upa-tirtha*, the *khanda*, the main *tirtha*, the *kshetra*, the *mandala*, and/or the *desha*.

To instance the above illustration: In Utkala *desha* (ancient name of Orissa) there are four *kshetras*,[29] namely, Yajpur or Jaipur as Parvati-kshetra (also Gada-kshetra), Konarka as Surya-kshetra (also Padma-kshetra), Bhuvaneshvara as Harakshetra, and Puri as Purushottama-kshetra (also Sri-kshetra and Sankha-kshetra). Under the Kashmira-mandala, there are several *kshetras*, such as Nandi-kshetra and Sureshvari-kshetra; of these the Sureshvari-kshetra enshrines a sacred spring known as the Gupta-Ganga *tirtha*. The Kashi-kshetra extends over two *yojanas* and a half from east to west and is half a *yojana* wide from north to south; out of this the Varanasi *tirtha* extend up to the river Asi; the *kshetra* is further divided into three *khandas*, each containing a number of *upa-tirthas*. The Gaya-kshetra is five *kroshas* in extent, Gaya *tirtha* is two *kroshas* and a half, and Gayasiras (Phalgu *upa-tirtha*) is only one *krosha*. Similar distinction between Prayaga-kshetra, Prayaga, and Triveni is made in the *Pauranic* description of these places.

The circumambulation on the seven holy circuits, namely, the *garbha-griha*, the *prakara*, the *antaragriha* (*khanda parikrama*), the *kshetra* (*panchakroshi parikrama*), the *mandala* (*chaurasi kroshi parikrama*), the *charodhama*, and the *saptapuri* makes the whole of India sacred. The pilgrim's recitation at every ritual that he is making a sacred performance in such and such *tirtha* under such and such *kshetra* located in the *Jamboo dwipe Bharata khande* is indeed the revelation of this concept of sacred India and a constant reminder that this should be treated so.

Organization of tirtha functionaries

The Brahmin priests officiating at the rites performed in a *tirtha* call themselves *Tirtha-purohita*, the priest of the *tirtha*. Since they accept donations and endowments at a *tirtha*, in defiance of the *sastric* injunction, they are relegated to a lower position. There are various types of priests engaged in pilgrim services, as pilgrim-guides and ritual associates. In Kashi, they are of such types:[30] the Tirtha-purohitas who receive the pilgrims at their residence and assist them in sacred performances; the Karmakandis who are competent priests for Vedic sacrifices; the Ghatias or the Ganga-putras (sons of the river Ganga) who assist the pilgrims in sacred performances at the ghats; the Bhaddars who escort the pilgrims from the railway station; and the Yatrawalas who guide and assist the pilgrims visiting temples. All these categories of priests and guides are popularly known as Panda. The priest of a temple, as distinguished from the priest engaged in pilgrim service, is called *Pujari*. The Mahapatras are those who officiate at the *sraddha* ritual. Among the ritual associates are the barbers, the musicians, the florists, the boatmen, and the Doms (the custodians of the sacred fire used in cremation).

Among the priests and guides of this kind we may mention such as:[31] the Sewayats of Puri; the Pandas of Deoghar, Gaya, Prayaga, Mathura, Badrinath, Kedarnath and Hardwara; the Divas connected with the Vallabhachari shrines of western India; the Sewakas of Pushakara; the Moylars connected with the Madhva temples of Tulu speaking region; the number of Karnataka; the Tantris and the Ambalavasis connected with the shrines of Malabar; the Dikshettars of Chidambaram; the Gurukkals and Bhattaras of Tamil Nadu; the Embrans of south Kanara; the Shivadhvajas, the Shivanambis, and the Tamball Shaivite priests of Karnataka; the Vaikhanasal of Andhra Pradesh; the Barna Brahmins of North India; the Agradani of Bengal; the Acharya of western India; and the Dakot of Sanichara Brahmins of Rajasthan who accept gifts of oil and sesame for propitiating the planet Saturn.

In South India, the contingent of temple functionaries[32] is large and complex. They are classed on the basis of such minute specialization in temple services as temple guards, sweeping the floor of the temple, decoration of the deity, preparing sandalwood paste, making wreath-ornament for the deity, the waving of lamps, worship and *abhiseka*, music and dance, recitation of the Vedas, cooking, offering food to the deity, and distribution of *prasada*, etc. The temple has its own potters, basket-makers, tailors, gardeners, carriers, and varieties of servants and specialists required in the organization of temple estate. Unlike the practice in the North, here there is no organization of pilgrim-services. Those who are associated with temples may also guide the pilgrims, but there is no separate category like the north-Indian Pandas, Bhaddars and Yatrawalas who are exclusively devoted to pilgrim services though unrelated to the temple organization.

Devadasis

Music and dance form a part of worship and ritual mostly in Shiva and Vishnu temples all over India. But the institution of Basavis and Devadasis or handmaids of gods, is peculiar to South India. The girls are dedicated to the temple in early childhood, they are married to God, not men. The priests train them in the art of dancing and singing, and their main duty is to dance and sing before the idols. In course of time the institution of Devadasis lost its grace and original purpose. Most Devadasis have now turned into prostitutes, and their sacred quarters crowding the *tirthas* are converted into brothels.

The tradition of music and dance in temples, however, continues. The *tirthas* associated with Krishna are the homes of *Rasa-lila* and various dances similar to it—all reminding the devotees of the loves of Krishna and the Gopis. In Gujarat the *garba* dance is performed in honour of the Goddess Durga, particularly during the Navaratra festival. It is on record that at the time of the plunder of Somanatha temple by Mahmud of Ghazni three hundred barbers used to share the pilgrims and three hundred and fifty dancing girls were at the service of the temple.

To sum up: The structure of the *tirthas* is built on the foundations of a wider concept which sustains the interest of the common people. The sacred space has been organized imaginatively, and a large contingent of specialists has been disposed towards pilgrim-services and the upkeep of the *tirthas* and the temple complexes. Because of efficient organization, the *tirthas* have held a powerful attraction not only for spiritual benefits but also for material gains. It is through the network of *tirthas* that a united India has been conceived and it is indeed the institution of *tirtha* which binds the people perpetually across the heterogeneous cultural geography of India

SACRED PERFORMANCES

Elaborate rules[33] regarding the eligibility (*adhikara*) for pilgrimage and the procedures to be observed by pilgrims have been laid down in the *Puranas* and the *Nibandhas*. Persons of all the four *varnas* and *ashramas*, both men and women, and a householder with his wife are allowed to undertake pilgrimage. Before starting on a pilgrimage one should keep fast, offer worship to Ganesh and *pitris*, honour good Brahmins, and then make a resolve (*sankalpa*) to go on pilgrimage. The pilgrimage should wear *karpatika* apparel, namely, a copper-ring, a copper bracelet, and a red robe. He should avoid making use of a conveyance drawn by men or bulls, or a chariot which is drawn by mules or horses, but he may use a boat to reach holy places like Gangasagara which cannot be reached otherwise. It has been provided that one should always go on a journey wearing shoes and holding an umbrella in the rains or in summer and also armed with a staff at night or in a forest. Tonsure and fast are acts that must be done at all *tirthas* except, according to some authorities, at Kurukshetra, Visala (Ujjaini or Badrika), Viraja (river in Orissa) and Gaya.

It may be mentioned here that the older rules of pilgrimage were comparatively simple, providing alternatives, but the later authorities made every ritual more elaborate and harder.

On reaching a *tirtha* the pilgrim is required to perform a number of rituals which may vary according to personal needs and prescribed customs of the place. Without going into the details of the modes of performances a few quaint and uncommon rituals associated with some *tirthas* may be recorded here.

Circumambulation

The clockwise circumambulation of a holy place or of several *tirthas* is believed to have the effects of a horse-sacrifice (*ashvamedha*). One of the most meritorious performances at Kashi is the *panchakroshi* pilgrimage—circumambulation of the holy *kshetra* with a radius of five *kroshas*. The 80 km *panchakroshi* road is journeyed in six days, visiting hundreds of shrines on foot. The pilgrims start from the Manikarnika and keeping to their right along the bank of the Ganga river cross the confluence of the dry river Asi and halt at the shrine of Kandava at a distance of about 8 km from the Manikarnika. The second halt is at Dhoopchandi, the third at Ramesvara, the fourth at Shivapur, the fifth at Kapildhara, and on the sixth day they move from Kapildhara to Varnasangam and thence to Manikarnika again. From there the pilgrims go to the temple of Sakshi-Vinayaka who is supposed to bear witness to this pilgrimage. The circumambulation of the three inner segments of Kashi, called *antaragrihi parikrama*, is equally meritorious. The ten-day circumambulation of Prayaga *mandala* is called *Vahiravedi-parikrama*, and the two-day circumambulation of its inner circuit is called *antaravedi-parikrama*. The *tirthas* like Naimisaranya, Janakpur, Ayodhya, Chitrakoot, Mathura-Vrindavana, Puri, Gaya, Girnar, Narmada and so on, have similar tradition of holy circumambulation.

There are also larger circuits of pilgrimage. The *chaurasi-kroshi parikrama* takes place on the radius of eightyfour *krosha* (267 km) from Kashi, and finally there is the circumambulation of *charodham* and *sapta-puri*, which completes the circuits of pilgrimage in India.

Going on a triangular pilgrimage is called *trikona-yatra*. In Vindhyachal, the nine-km *trikona-yatra* is endowed with special merit. Throughout India there is a universal practice of *pradakshina*—going round the idol of the deity, the *garbha-griha*, the *antaramandala*, and even the outermost wall of the temple precinct.

Kshetra-sannyas

In the somewhat grotesque imagery of the *Puranas*, a pilgrim to Kashi is recommended to break his legs on a stone, so that they may not run away with him from the holy city. The central idea is to live in Kashi till death. As stated, the vow to dwell within the sacred territory of a *tirtha* till death is called *kshetra-sannyas*. The person who has taken this vow must not cross the boundaries of the *tirtha* even for religious purposes, A *kshetra-sannyasi* in Kashi is interdicted from undertaking the *panchakroshi* circumambulation. His salvation is already secured, and no further pilgrimage is required.

In Kashi, people from all over India come with the expressed purpose of leading religious life and to die in the holy city. They may not follow the rules of *kshetra-sannyas*, and yet their salvation is guaranteed. It is mostly the old and the widows who come here for what is called *kashi-vasa* –living in Kashi permanently with the religious motive.

Garbha-vasa

To dwell in a *tirtha* for nine months with a vow not to cross its sacred territory is called *garbha-vasa.* Living in a holy place for nine months is like living in the mother's womb (*garbha*), and hence this duration of pilgrimage is called *garbha-vasa.* The one who has performed this efficacious rite is freed from the cycle of rebirth.

Kalpa-vasa

Staying in a *tirtha*, usually on the bank of a holy river, for one month is called *kalpa-vasa.* In Prayaga, bathing at the *sangama* for the whole month of Magha is endowed with inexhaustible merits. It is said that even three days bath at the *sangama* is equal to the gift of three crores of cows.

Austerities

Fasting, sexual continence, abstinence from unguents, soft-bed and luxuries, rejection of the aid of vehicles or animals for making journey, and walking without shoes in *tirthas* are some of the practices enjoyed on the pilgrims.

Measuring of the length of the pilgrim's body by successive prostration on the ground as he journeys to the sacred place is one of the most difficult performances. This is called *danda-pranama.*

The holy bath

The holy bath is an essential purificatory rite for all kinds of sacred performances. It may also be performed independently as a ritual complete in itself. A holy bath in the Ganga secures merits—purifies and frees from sins at once, and yields heaven and *moksha.* By bathing in the Ganga and drinking its water one purifies one's family up to the seventh ancestor.

Bathing in holy rivers is always meritorious. But on some occasions, usually connected with astronomical conjunctions, every river and tank gains the virtue of the Ganga, and the Ganga and other all-time holy rivers must, therefore, be much more efficacious than usual. One such occasion is known as *ardhodaya.* It occurs when in the month of Magha or Pausa, a new-moon falls on Sunday, and the rising constellation is *shravana* (during day time) and the *yoga* is *vyatipata.* Eclipses of the sun and the moon are similar occasions when a miraculous transformation of the nature of waters takes place.

Another combination which requires the conjunction of the planet Jupiter with other planets has been shown in Table 3.1. It happens only once in twelve years at four places, namely, Hardwara, Prayaga, Ujjain and Nasik. The occasion is called *kumbha*. Six years before and after each *kumbha mela* comes *ardha-kumbha*. The *ardha-kumbha* takes place only at Hardwara and Prayaga. The occasion of *kumbha* attracts immense numbers of bathers from all parts of India. It is however considered as the festival of ascetics, because on this occasion the naked ascetics (*naga-sannyasis*) have preference in the priority of bathing at the holy spot.

TABLE 3.1 : Showing the occurrence of Kumbha

Place	*Month*	*Position of planets*	
Hardwara	March-April	Jupiter × Aquarius	Kumbha
Prayaga	December-January	Jupiter × Aries	
		Sun × Capricorn	Kumbha
Nasik	July-September	Jupiter × Leo	Kumbha
Ujjain	May-June	Jupiter × Leo	Kumbha

Religious suicide

Suicide has generally been condemned by the authorities on *Dharmasastras*, but some exceptions to this are made in such cases:[34] (a) by those guilty of *mahapatakas* (namely Brahman murder, drinking of *sura*, theft of Brahman's gold, and incest); (b) by a forest hermit suffering from incurable diseases and unable to perform the duties of his order; (c) by an old man or one who cannot observe the rules of bodily purification or who is so ill as to be beyond medical skill; (d) by a householder if his life's work is done, if he has no desire for the pleasures of the world and does not desire to live, or if he is a Vedantin and convinced of the ephemeral nature of life; (e) by a wife dying by *sahagamana* or *anumarana;* and (f) by religious suicide at some *tirthas*.

Religious suicide is allowed at Prayaga, Gangasagara, Purusottama-kshetra, Kashi, Prthudaka, Srisaila, at the confluence of Narmada and Kaveri and also at Amarkantaka.

The meritorious modes of suicide are such : (1) starving; (2) covering oneself with dry cowdung cakes and setting it on fire and consuming oneself therein; (3) burying oneself in snow; (4) to plunge into water at the *sangam*, enumerate one's sins and pray till alligators come and devour the man; (5) hanging with head down in the stream and feet up and drinking the waters of the Ganga; (6) cut one's own throat, or cutting off one's own flesh and giving it as food to birds; and (7) by falling head-long from a cliff, at Amarkantaka, for instance.

Religious suicide was considered as one of the approved and undoubted means of securing *moksha*, heaven and similar reward. But gradually this became one of the forbidden acts of Kali age, or what is called *kalivarjya*. Some of the later medieval writers, however, upheld this practice with some reservation. For instance, Narayanabhatta (born in A.D. 1513) writes (about A.D. 1580) in his great scholarly work *Trishthalisetu* that one may resort to suicide at Prayaga for the attainment of *moksha*, but no one has authority to do so after abandoning to their fate one's old parents, young wife and children that require support, nor should a woman who is pregnant or who has young children or who has no permission from her husband.

Animal-sacrifice

The sacrificing of animals constituted an important item of Vedic ritual. The greatest of the Vedic sacrifices was the horse-sacrifice. Animal-sacrifice (*pasu-yaga*) prevailed in Vedic times, and even cow-sacrifice (*gomedha* or *gosava*) is prescribed in the Vedas. The sacrifice of the spit-ox (*sula-gava*) for propitiating Rudra and averting plague in cattle was also performed. Now the cow-sacrifice is a prohibited practice, *kalivarjya*. The horse-sacrifice was performed even in medieval times. And in *tirthas* like Varanasi, Gaya, Ganga, Godavari, Narmada, Prayaga, Mathura and Kurukshetra the sacred-spot where ten horses were once sacrificed is identified today, each having Dasasvamedha as a *upa-tirtha*.

The sacrifice (*bali*) of goats, sheep and buffaloes is essential for the propitiation of Shakta deities. It is widely prevalent in the *tirthas* of eastern India such as Kamakhya and Kalighat.

The number of victims sacrificed and the flow of blood on each day, particularly on a ceremonial day, make the *tirtha* more terrifying than pleasant. There are elaborate rituals of slaughtering the consecrated animal. The flesh of the sacrificial animal is eaten as *mahaprasada*, and even the vegetarian devotees wear the holy-mark of the sacrificial blood.

Some non-brahmanic deities are propitiated best by bloody sacrifice of pigs, fowl and pigeons.

The killing of the sacrificial animal is prohibited at the *tirthas* under strong Vaishnava influence. In such places, after performing a symbolic sacrifice the animal is let loose to wander at will. One may also cut a *kalabash* fruit imagining it to be a buffalo, or break coconuts in lieu of bloody sacrifice. It may be noted here that the breaking of coconuts as ritual offering to gods and goddesses is widely prevalent in places where animal sacrifice is prohibited. The offering of the effigy of a horse made of clay or of cloth is a popular ritual at the non-Brahmanic shrines in different parts of India, particularly in western India.

Animal-worship

Consecrated bulls, cows and monkeys are fed and worshipped at all *tirthas* sacred to Shiva and Vishnu. In the *tirthas* associated with death rituals, one of the most important ceremonies is the *vrisotasarga*. The ceremony takes place on the full-moon day in Kartika or Asvina. A dark coloured bull with all auspicious marks is brought, and the blacksmith brands the bull, on one flank with a discus and on the other flank with a trident. The bull is then washed and decked; four young cows are brought to him as his beloved to roam about sportingly. The bull is thus let loose in the *tirtha* and worshipped by the pilgrims as *Nandi*—the vehicle of Shiva. It is because of this practice that Kashi gives a look of a pastoral city. Most *tirthas* associated with Rama and Krishna such as Ayodhya, Chitrakoot and Vrindavana are the cities of monkeys—the tribesmen of Hanuman who was the ardent devotee of Rama. In places like Hardwara, Martanda, Vrindavana and Ayodhya one of the common sacred performances is to offer food to fish and tortoise living in the holy waters. The places sacred to Krishna are the abodes of holy cows, peacocks and pigeons. In Deshanoka, a holy place near Bikaner, there is a temple of Karnijee, the family deity of the Rathors, where rats are reared and goats sacrificed. There are countless rats called the *kabe* of Karnijee and they are propitiated by offering sweets.

The worship of serpent is widely prevalent in India. In the Kashmir valley, Anantanaga is the *tirtha* sacred to the king of the serpent God Ananta. On the way Kedarnath, there is a holy place called Garuda-chatti which is associated with Garuda mythical combination of the bird Garuda and man—the vehicle of Vishnu. There is also a Hansa *tirtha* in the Himalayas, sacred to the goose—the charger of Brahma. The Kapota *tirtha* under Godavari, Kapotaka *tirtha* under Sabbramati, and Kapotesvara under Sriparvata are associated with the pigeon.

Tonsure of women

The authorities are divided in their opinion on the religious necessity of tonsure of women[35] in holy places. According to one view only widows have to tonsure their heads, and the women whose husband is living may cut only two or three finger breadths of her tresses. The other view is that women should not tonsure their head at any *tirtha* except at Prayaga, and there too only after obtaining the permission of their husbands. Tirupati is another *tirtha* where the complete tonsure of the head for both men and women is a common practice.

Pinda-dana

The offering of *pindas* (propitiatory rites to the manes) at holy places is an obligatory ritual. There are fiftyfive *tirthas* (according to some, 168) meritorious for performing the rites of *sraddha*. They are called *pitri-tirthas*. Of these, Gaya is the most important *pitri-tirtha* and Ganga the *pitri-nadi* where the fruit of offerings made is inexhaustible. In Gaya it is obligatory for a man to offer *pinda* to his ancestors to save them from hell, and even to himself but without sesame. An ascetic (*sannyasi*) should not offer *pindas* but should merely exhibit (hold up) his staff and should put it down on Vishnupada at Gaya. There are elaborate rules and modes of performing *sraddha:* "At Gaya, one may offer (to *pitris*) *pindas* by means of *payasa* (rice cooked in milk), boiled rice, barley flour, fruits and roots, the cake of sesame (after oil is extracted), sweetmeats or jaggery with *ghee* or with curds alone or with invigorating honey. In a *sraddha* at Gaya, the procedure consists in preparing a seat for the *pindas*, the offering of *pindas*, the sprinkling of water again (on the *kusa* grass), giving fees and declaration of dinner (to Brahmans); but there is no invocation of *pitris*, no curtains of privacy and no blemish due to *sraddha* being seen (by undesirable persons or animals)".[36] It is believed that Gaya is the appropriate *tirtha* for performing *sraddha* in respect of male ancestors; for the female ancestors Siddhapur in north Gujarat is the fit place, and hence it is called *Matri-Gaya.*

Miscellaneous tirtha practices

Holy bath, vows, prayer, worship, waving of *arti* (lamp), gift, *godana* (gifting of cow), and *tarpana* (water oblation to *pitris*) and *prayaschita* (penance and ritual purification) are recommended for performances at every *tirtha.* Several other performances which pilgrims are supposed to make according to the commended practice of a *tirtha,* may briefly be recorded as follows:

Ceremonial throwing of milk, flowers, coconuts, fruits, betel-leaves, betel-nuts and money into holy rivers is considered meritorious.

Throwing of the bones which remain after cremation into holy rivers is specially recommended for conferring *moksha* on the dead. This is called *asthi visarjana.*

Sweeping the streets of Kashi is a meritorious act.

Branding the pilgrim's body with a red-hot metal stamp containing the impressions of discus and conch of Vishnu is enjoined at Dwarka. This is called *dama* or *chhapa.*

Kashi is called *mahashamshana*—the great cremation ground. The cremation at this place secures *moksha.* Hence the dead bodies and the dying persons from far-off places are hurriedly brought to Kashi for cremation at the Manikarnika. This is called the pilgrimage of the dead and the dying.

One of the peculiar features of the Purushottama *tirtha*[37] at Puri is that in the court of the Jagannatha and outside the

Lion Gate no distinction of caste is observed. The second special feature is that the holy rice cooked as offering to Jagannath is regarded as so sanctified that all barriers of caste are transcended. A Puri priest will receive the holy food even from a low caste Hindu. The feeling is that cooked rice when once placed before Jagannath never ceases to be pure. Hence the *mahaprasada* is dried and taken to all parts of India. At the periodical *shraddha* among Vaishnavas a grain of this holy rice is invariably put on the cake as the most sacred article that can be offered to the manes. Such exceptional treatment of *prasada* (sharing the holy food by Chandala and Brahmin without making any distinction of pure-impure) can be seen also at Bhuvaneshvara and Badrinath.

The offerings of food and drink of various kinds are made according to the specific requirements of gods and goddesses: Shiva is propitiated best by the water from the river Ganga, milk, honey and *bhanga* (*cannabis sativa*); the Shakta deities are pleased by flesh and wine. The god Saturn is offered salt and oil, the Vaishnava deities are fond of sweets and clarified butter. One of the essential offerings at the great shrine of Badrinath is horse-gram.

Among various other articles of offerings, we may list pieces of cloth, flags, tri-colour (red-yellow-white) or black threads, vermilion, sandalwood paste, incense, *durba* grass and flowers. The effigy of an umbrella or a crown made of silver or gold (called *chhatra*) is offered usually to a female deity. In eastern India the female deities are sometimes offered a basket-like pendant structure made of reeds. The pilgrims from Puri and Dwarka return home with cane-sticks. The offering of cane-sticks to gods is peculiar to the shrines associated with the cult of Krishna. The conch-shells are also offered at the Vaishnava shrines.

Pilgrimage is considered efficacious in the fulfilment of the three cardinal desires—*putreshana* (desire for son), *Vitteshana* (desire for wealth), and *lokeshana* (desire for worldly gains). Some of the *tirthas* are specially approachable for removing barrenness or for having male child. The *linga* at Baidyanath-dhama is called *manokamanalinga* which can be propitiated for the fulfilment of all desires, including the desire to have a child. The woman desirous of an offspring takes a bath in the Shiva-ganga tank usually with her husband, and then they lie down on the verandah performing a fast for three days and three nights. This is called *dharna* or *kusothar*. During this time the grace of God is indicated to her or the husband in a dream. Following this the woman marks the wall of the temple with red impression by both her hands upside down. This is called *chhapa*. When the desire is fulfilled, she comes back to make another impression of her hands, but this time in upright direction. She also erects a flag-staff and fastens the spire of the temple of Shiva and Parvati with a long coloured thread.

Another peculiar practice at this holy shrine of the Lord Baidyanath is reported as such : A person in need of money observes *dharna*, and on the third night a leaf of *pipal* tree is left in the temple. The following morning when the temple gates are opened, the priest finds the order of the Lord written there, addressed to some rich man for payment of the sum in favour of the person who is praying. The priest copies this on a piece of paper and hands over to the person who has prayed for it. This is known as the *hundi* of Baba Baidyanath. The man upon whom this *hundi* or cheque is drawn dares not to disobey.

The *dharna* is performed also for the cure of diseases. Baidyanath is also the Lord of medicine, and hence person suffering from chronic diseases make special pilgrimage to this place. Several other *tirthas* are famous for curing disease. The believers are said to be cured of leprosy by the grace of Adi-Gadadhara Vishnu at Gaya, by holy bath in the hot spring at Rajgir, and by propitiating the sun god at Konarak.

Sexual intercourse at a *tirtha* is prohibited. But on the bank of the river Jeebachha in north Bihar, there is a festival of "child-bearing" when after taking a holy bath the couples cohabit right there with a view to increasing fertility.

Festivals

In every *tirtha*, the *mahotsava* (ceremonies and festivals) associated with the deities of the place are observed periodically. These attract pilgrims from far-off places in large numbers. A *tirtha* may be observing some of the festivals in common with the other *tirthas* but may also be having its own special feature. The birth or marriage anniversary of gods and goddesses is celebrated at many *tirthas*. The *Ramnavmi* at Ayodhya, the *Vivaha-panchami* at Janakpur, the *Krishna-janmastami* at Mathura and Dwarka, the *Shivaratri* and the *Annakoota* at Kashi, and the *Dasahara* at Kalighat and Kamakhya are special occasions of pilgrimage. The colourful ceremony of *Jhoolan* in which the idol swings for a number of days is common with the shrines associated with Krishna. The ceremony of carrying out the idol round the *tirtha* in a palanquin, accompanied by music and procession, is a usual sight at the *tirthas* in south India.

The festival of taking round the deity in a wooden car drawn by male and female devotees is also one of the most celebrated events at some *tirthas*. In Puri the festival called *Ratha-yatra*[38] starts on the 2nd day of the bright half of *Asadh*. The car of Jagannath is about 45 feet in height, 35 feet square, and is supported on 16 wheels of 7 feet diameter with 16 spokes in each and has Garuda as a crest; the second car is that of Subhadra, which is a little smaller than Jagannath's car, resting on 12 wheels with 12 spokes in each and having a *padma* (lotus) as the crest; the third car is that of Balarama resting on 14 wheels and 14 spokes in each wheel and has Hanuman for crest. The cars are drawn by pilgrims and hired labourers from the temple to the country house of Jagannath (which is about two miles away), amidst the shouts and emotional songs of thousands of pilgrims. On the 10th day of the bright-half begins the return of the cars from the country house. This is the most important festival of Puri considered as the special feature of Jagannath. Elsewhere also, particularly in south India, the car-festival is of significance, yielding great merit.

The constraints of space will not permit even a brief account of the major sacred performances, and hence this exploratory venture to glance at the grand-sweep of the history of *tirtha*-practices must end here and now with the following observations: The sacred performances are many and various. The diversities of performances both in time and in space offer a wide range of choice to people of diverse cultures. The obligatory performances such as *pindadana* and *parikrama*, promote a strong cultural linkage between the regions and the people of India.

DIVERSITIES IN TRADITIONS

Clearly, the purpose of this essay is served if the foregoing pages have conveyed an impression of the vastness and complexity of the subject. The following pages illustrate the feasibility and importance of analysing the cultural diversities of *tirthas* which the anthropologists of religion have so far neglected. In concluding the tradition of *tirthas*, we shall, therefore, look briefly at several different levels of diversities.

Diversities of categories

As stated, there are various textual categories of holy places created by the diversity of conceptions. First, there is the geographical category based on the natural form of a *tirtha* such as *sagar* (sea), *dwipa* (island), *nadi* (river), *kunda* (wells), *sarovara* and *pushkara* (lakes and tanks), *dhara* (fountains), *agni-kunda* (hot-spring), *parvata* (hills), *aranya* (forests) and *puris* (towns).

The second category is formed on the basis of territorial limits. The *mandala*, the *kshetra*, the *tirtha*, the *khanda* and the *upa-tirtha* are distinguishable in extent, each subsequent one being smaller and holier than each preceding one.

The third category relates to the functional aspect of holy places. Thus there are *siddha-kshetra*, *mukti-kshetra*, *pitri-tirtha*, and even *pasu-tirtha* like Kolyata where animals after succumbing to death attain salvation.

The fourth category of holy places is formed on the basis of their association with the principal gods and goddesses. There are Vishnu-kshetra, Shiva-kshetra, Surya-kshetra, Brahma-kshetra, Parvati-kshetra, Ganapatya-kshetra, and the like.

The fifth category denotes their origin, and hence all the holy places are placed under the four-fold division, namely, *daiva*, *asura*, *arsa* and *manusa*.

The sixth category makes a trichotomic division of *tirthas* into *jangam*, *sthavara* and *manas*.

The seventh category puts a number of *tirthas* into special classes such as the *chaturdhama*, the *saptapuri*, the *pitha* and the *Jyotirlinga*.

Diversity of performances

The diversity of sacred performances is created by the variety of contexts and the diversity of cultures. There are various contexts such as *samskaric* (associated with life-crises), *parmarthic* (spiritual), and *vyavaharic* (worldly desires—*vitteshana*, *putreshana* and *lokeshana*). In each of these contexts there are varieties of performances, and the modes, objects, and offerings of each performance may vary according to textual prescription and oral tradition. In respect of the scrupulous details of a performance there may be individual, caste, sect, and cultural variations.

Such variations in the performances may occur in a single sacred spot, or in a cluster of sacred spots, or in a large segment, or in the sacred zone of a *tirtha* containing numerous *upa-tirthas*. A detailed description of the varieties of traditions in sacred performances at a major intra-*tirtha* level has been attempted elsewhere.[39] A similar attempt may be made to work out the nature and the range of variation at the inter-*tirtha* level. Such a venture will, of course, have to wait for the data from different *tirthas* in a systematized form.

Diversity of the performers

The diversity as reflected in different levels of cultures of the performers provides at once a wider and deeper understanding of the tradition of *tirthas* as also of the civilization which has made them what they are. This point has been illustrated elsewhere[40] comprehensibly; here the basis of its conceptual formulation may be referred to briefly.

An empirical study of Kashi shows that all the pilgrims visiting the holy city do not participate in its sacred complex equally. The extent of participation depends largely on the pilgrims' cultural knowledge of a *tirtha* and of the textual prescriptions regarding the rituals to be performed there. Hence the participation of the pilgrims belonging to Oral, Textual, and Transcendental Cultural Traditions (in the *tirthas* embodying varieties of Brahmanic and non-Brahmanic sacred traditions) will be necessarily unequal. Thus, a potter pilgrim belonging to the Oral Cultural Tradition feels satisfied if a Brahmin priest takes him to the shrine of Vishwanath in Kashi for worship and to the river Ganga for a holy bath. The priest may take him to some other Brahmanic shrines, but that does not form an essential part of his pilgrimage. What is really important for him and what he does on his own is to visit the non-Brahmanic shrine such as Agiyabir where he is himself competent to perform such rites as to cure himself from a chronic disease he may be suffering from, or to have an offspring. His participation in the Brahmanic sacred complex of Kashi is only minimal and peripheral. Where he interacts more freely and closely are the places which have no scriptural sanction and which lie outside the sacred geography of Kashi. The Brahmin pilgrim belonging to the Textual Cultural Tradition, on the other hand, tries to visit all the sacred shrines and to perform all the rituals enjoined by the *shastras* to the best of his means. But a Dandi *sannyasi* belonging to the Transcendental Cultural Tradition may or may not perform any ritual in Kashi. Since he is an Advaitin he is not supposed to believe in gods and goddesses, and hence his visit to a temple is not only unnecessary but also inconsistent with his spiritual ideals. At the time of taking *sannyas* he had performed his own funeral rite which symbolizes his "death" as an individual in this world, and, therefore, he is no longer required to be guided by "this-worldly" laws. To him ideally there is no distinction between what people call "sacred" and "profane". His visit to a place of pilgrimage may, therefore, be casual or motivated by personal reasons. Ideally his participation in the pilgrimage, in the sense of ritual performances, is practically nil.

Thus, the three persons belonging to three different cultural traditions interact with *tirthas* differently and in unequal extents.

Diversity of regional cultures

The diversity of *tirthas* derives from the diversity of regional cultures. The Indian sub-continent is well-known for its geographic, racial and linguistic diversities. Different regions of India have evolved distinct cultures[41] in respect of the material art of life as also of the finer forms of culture, namely, art and architecture, dance and music. Even in classical culture and the Brahmanic social and ritual organization[42] this kind of regionality emerges prominently. Here are a few examples of regionality in the organization of sacred traditions.

On the basis of temple types, India may be roughly marked into two parts, the North and the South. The local specialization further marks off western and central India from eastern India, and the Tamil-speaking area from Karnataka, Andhra and Orissa. The gigantic construction and imposing *gopuras* which mark the temples in other parts of south India are conspicuous by their absence in Kerala.

Each large region has only one or two favourite gods. From central Uttar Pradesh to Bihar, Rama is the favourite idol of the people; in western India it is Krishna who commands popularity. Maharashtra and Karnataka commonly worship Vithoba. Parthasarthi is adored in Tamil Nadu, while Narsingh has many devotees in Andhra Pradesh. Each region has one or two important regional shrines. Guravayura and Padmanabha temples in Kerala; Madurai and Srirangam in Tamil Nadu; Chamundesvari and Udipi in Karnataka; Tirupati in Andhra Pradesh; Pandharpur in Maharashtra; Dakora in Gujarat; Nathadware in Rajasthan; Shanta Durge and Mangesh in Goa; Ambika or Arasur and Jalandhara in Punjab; Vaishnava Devi in Jammu, Ksheera Bhavani and Anantanaga in Kashmir; Jawalamukhi, Mandi and Chamba in Himachal Pradesh; Hardwar in western Uttar Pradesh, Vindhyachal in eastern Uttar Pradesh; Baidyanathdhama in Bihar; Bhubaneshwar in Orissa; Tarkeshvara and Kalighat in Bengal; and Kamaroopa-Kamakhya in Assam.

The modes of sacred performances have considerable regional variations. If eastern India follows the Tantrika modes of worship, the other parts of India practise the Vaidika form. Kerala[43] has evolved a system which combines the Vaidika and the Tantrika modes, and, therefore, in Kerala Tantra is looked upon as a distinct *prasthana* in itself.

Every region observes distinctive religious and social customs, both positive and negative, called *achura* and *anachara*. Not much work has been done on this important aspect of

Indian tradition, but some of the *anacharas* of Kerala[44] are certainly distinct from the rest of the country.

The scriptural modes of worship and the canons of social usages may differ according to the Vedic *Sakhas*, *Smritis* and *Sutras*. And since different regions follow different texts, the difference in rituals and social customs is bound to perpetrate. Thus the diversity of regional cultures is built up not only by the non-Brahmanic local traditions but also by the Brahmanic scriptures.

Distribution of culture traits

If culture traits of the *tirthas* are plotted on the map of India the North-South divide would become amply clear. The lack of adequate data may not permit a thorough treatment of the subject, but we may examine here the distribution pattern of, at least, a few relatively known traits.

(1) Creating a *tirtha* by deifying land or natural objects: A large area is sanctified as *tirtha*. It retains its sacred character permanently. The sacred dwellings such as temples built on this place are of lesser significance. When temples in Kashi were destroyed by the Pathan and Moghul rulers, the *tirtha* maintained its sanctity irreducibly. It is said that there is not even as much space as a sesame seed in Kashi which has not a *linga* (the emblem of Shiva); every dust particle of this place is sacred. Thus, the sacred is in-built with the natural objects and places, and hence the importance of geographic categories and the concepts like *mandala*, *kshetra*, etc.

This trait of deifying a horizontal space is peculiar to north India.

(2) The creation of a *tirtha* by building temples and housing the god is largely a south Indian tradition. The large temple complex and the walled sacred territory are the characteristic features of the South. The space outside the walled temple of Meenakshi in Madurai is not as sacred (or at all sacred) as the space outside the temple of Vishwanath in Kashi. Hence, the concepts like *mandala* and *kshetra* are of little relevance in south India.[45] The gradation of sacred space is made there by concentric walls built around the main temple. What is most significant there in the sacred geography is the temple structure and within this the

garbhagriha, the *prakara*, and the *gopura*. The *gopura* at the entrance of the temple has to be necessarily majestic and a replica of the entire sacred complex, because it is the gateway of the sacred, which people must see from a long distance. The *most sacred* space is the *sanctum sanctorum*.

This trait of deifying a vertical space is typically south Indian.

(3) The trait of circumambulating a large tract derives from the trait of deifying a horizontal space. Hence the north Indian custom of *panchakroshi* or *chaurasikroshi-parikrama* is absent in the South.

(4) Organizing a large number of shrines spread over in a large area and the varieties of sacred performance to be made in each of these shrines would demand a large number of specialists of various kinds such as pilgrim guides, pilgrim-priests specialized in different types of rituals, and several others associated with ritual services. Hence the organization of pilgrim services such as the institution of Pandas and the allied groups is an important element in north Indian *tirthas*.

(5) The contingent of temple functionaries of various kinds will be comparatively large in south India, because there the temple services have to be organized scrupulously.

(6) The nature of temple organization in south India necessitates the elaboration of worship and rituals largely connected with the life-cycle of gods and goddesses. There are various categories of temple-priests organized in hierarchical order, functionaries of various kinds associated with the management of food, decoration, recreation and visitation of the deity. This calls for the institution of Devadasis, heavy instrumental music in temple rituals, the practice of taking round the deity in a palanquin or a chariot, the celebration of *utsavas* of various kinds, and even the trait of constructing spacious *mandapa* for dance and music and the *deepa-stambha* for decoration of light.

(7) Clustering of heterogeneous shrines, organizing *tirthas* within a *tirtha*, temples within a temple, and sharing a common space by the idols of different gods and goddesses belonging to different sects are the characteristic features of the north Indian *tirthas*.

(8) Distancing the heterogeneous shrines, keeping the gods and goddesses of different sects at a distance, is typically a south Indian trait. The sectarian distinction between the Shaivites and the Vaishnavites in south India is conspicuous and wide.

From the distribution of the *tirtha* traits (Map) it appears that south India has built up a tradition distinct from the North. Orissa in the east and Goa in the west seem to be a meeting ground of the two traditions. Such interpenetration of the northern and the southern traditions can be found in these eastern and western regions in other items of culture as well.

UNITY IN DIVERSITIES

Unity in diversities is the essence of India's cultural traditions. Despite all the diversities, just mentioned, there is an over-all unity of belief and practices at all levels. For instance, "in spite of local differentiation, the underlying ideas that guided the symbolic meaning of temple-forms were common between the North and the South. The significance of the images continued to be subject to the same ideals as before, though the artistic traditions under which these were executed differed widely".[46] In all the various forms of music and dance there is a unity of themes and melodic patterns and cadences. Similarly, whatever may be the variation in the modes of organizing the sacred, the source which holds them together is the body of Brahmanic scriptures.

Every civilization has its own method of handling diversities. Thus, while Semitic civilizations lay stress on the unification of characteristics, Sanskritic civilization, on the contrary, allows the diversities to perpetuate. The contrariety in the two modes of integration flows from the difference in the basic philosophy of the two systems concerning the knowledge of the sacred. For instance, while Semitic religions like Islam and Christianity claim to have revealed *the* truth, Sanskritic religion (popularly known as Hinduism or Brahmanism) profess no such revelation. The Hindu view is that the 'whole truth' is unknowable, and it is only the 'part truth' which may be known by mortals. Consequently there

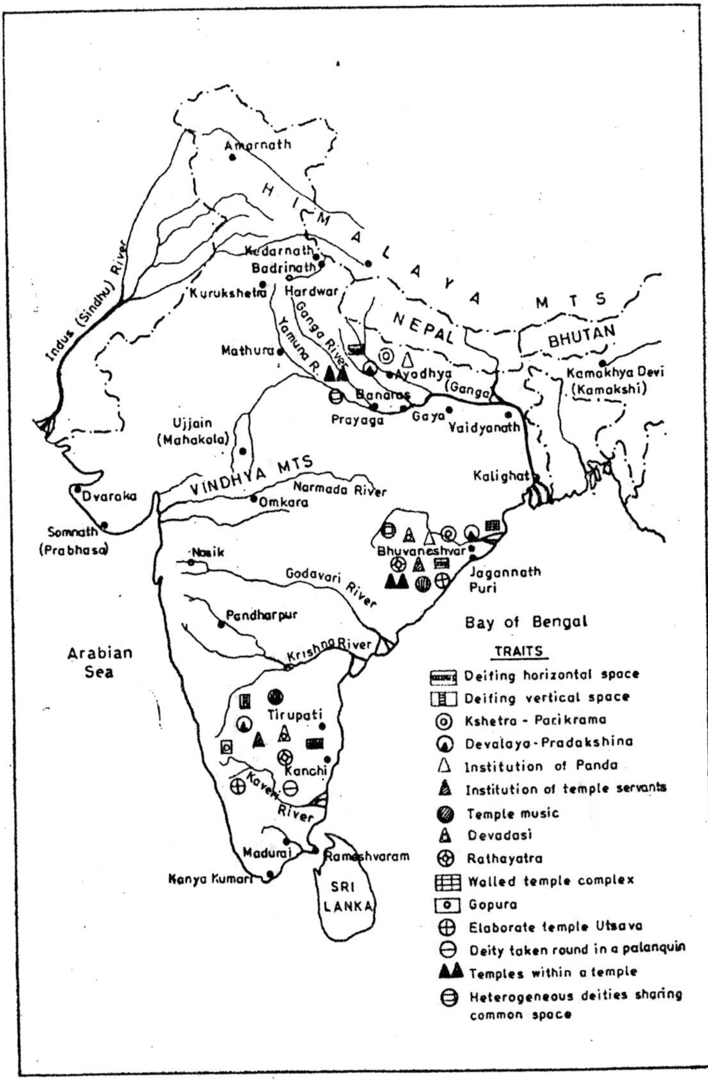

Sketch map of India : Showing the distribution of Tirtha-traits

are different paths which lead to the Truth and one can journey along any path one chooses. This freedom of belief and practices is clearly reflected in the conception of gods and the modes of devotion and worship. There is the nine-fold path of devotion known as *navadhabhakti* and one can follow any branch thereof according to one's ability and aptitude. Brahmanism is perhaps the only religion which says that even enmity towards God may lead to the attainment of salvation. The diversity is only in the means, the end being the same, namely, the attainment of God.

Philosophical explanation apart, there have been conscious efforts to level down the diversities of regional traditions by establishing the sacred institution of *tirthas*. Although each region developed its own regional *tirtha*, built up around the local myths, yet the different regions of India were linked by establishing supra-regional *tirthas* and by inventing the myth of *avatara* which reduces all forms of regional gods and goddesses into universal Trinity. Thus, the four *dhamas* and the four *pithas* of the Adya Shankaracharya at the cardinal points and the twelve *Jyotirlingas*, the 108 Shakta *pithas*, the 168 *pitri-tirthas*, the seven *moksha-dayani puris*, and all the great rivers and mountains and oceans establish an intimate sacred network of relationship between the peoples of diverse regional cultures.

The luminaries who built up the institution of *tirtha* have enjoined *tirtha-padayatra* (journeying to the holy places on foot) to ensure that the pilgrims interact closely with the peoples of different regions, traversing intensively and extensively, thus keeping up the currents of civilization in constant circulation. Even the traditionally prohibited places such as Anga, Vanga, Kalinga, Sauvira and Magadha were allowed for purposes of pilgrimage. Thus, virtually the whole of India was brought within the field of *tirtha-yatra*—the wide spectrum of the sacred journey.

For the benefit of those who are unable to travel any long distance on pilgrimage, the *tirtha* comes to their door. And hence, there is a Dakshina-Kashi in the South, a Uttara-Kashi and Gupta-Kashi in the northern Himalaya, a Gupta-Kashi in the east in Bhubaneshwara, a western Kashi in Nasik (also Paithan) in Maharashtra, and one more Kashi in

Mandi in the western Himalaya. Pilgrimage to each of these places is endowed with the merits of the sacred journey attached to the Kashi of Vishwanath in Uttar Pradesh. The *Puranas* hold that Kashi and Kanchi are like the two eyes of Shiva. Similarly there are several Ganga rivers, each flowing in a large area and thus covering the whole of India. The one who is physically incapable to bathe even in the nearby Ganga may drink its water or just remember it in order to be freed from sins at once. The *Vishnu Purana* (II.8.120-1) says: The Ganga purifies all beings from day to day when its name is heard, when one desires to see it, when it is seen or touched, or when its waters are drunk, or when one plunges into it, or when one utters or sings its name; when people utter the name 'Ganga' even though living at a distance of hundreds of *yojanas*, their sins, accumulated in three births, are destroyed. Hence Ganga is accessible everywhere, in all circumstances.

Similarly, the practice of throwing *asthis* in all the major rivers throughout the country and remembering one's ancestors by performing *sraddha* in different *tirthas* spread all over the land is the positive technique of holding the peoples of distant places together. Thus, no part of India is left unassociated with the loving memory of one's ancestors.

In conclusion, it is the institution of *tirtha* which, in an intensity beyond measure, binds this vast and varied country. There is nothing that can truly replace this natural and spontaneous sacred institution in its harmonious function of promoting the most sustainable unity.

NOTES

1. See, Saraswati (1975).
2. See, *A Comparative Dictionary of the Indo-Aryan Languages*, R.L. Turner (1966), Oxford; *Pali-English Dictionary*, T.W. Rhys Davids and William Stede (1959), London.
3. See, *Brhaddharma Purana* (5), cf. Hazra (1963: 404).
4. Cf., *The Institutes of Vishnu* (LXII.1-4); see also *The Institutes of Manu* (II. 58-59).
5. See, *Brhaddharma Purana* (5, 24), cf. Hazra, *op. cit.*, pp. 404, 409.

6. *Ibid.*, p. 404.
7. See, *Padma Purana* (II.39, 56-61), cf. Kane (1953: 564).
8. See, *Brhaddharma Purana* (7), cf. Hazra, *op. cit.*, p. 401.
9. Kane, *op. cit.*, pp. 534-5.
10. May the divine waters be weal for us, for our help and for our drink, weal and health may they bring unto us. (*Rig Veda* X.9.4). See also, *Rig Veda* VIII.47.49, X.9.30.
11. Forth from the Hills of snow they stream, and meet in Sindhu here or there.

    To me the sacred waters gave the balm that heals the heart's disease.

    Whatever rupture I have had that injured eyes or heels or toes. All this the Waters, skilfulest physicians, shall make well again.

    All Rivers who have Sindhu for your Lady, Sindhu for your Queen.

    Give us the balm that heals this ill, this boon let us enjoy from you. (*Atharva Veda*, VI.24.1-3).

    Auspicious be the firmly seated Mountains, auspicious be the Rivers and Waters. (*Atharva Veda*, XIX.10.8).

    May stainless waters cleanse us from defilement.

    May they carry sin away from us, may they carry away from us the evil dream.

    Look on me with a friendly eye,
    O Waters, and touch my skin
    With your auspicious body (*Atharva Veda*, XVI.1.10-2)
12. See Kane, *op. cit.*, pp. 562-4.
13. *Ibid.*, pp. 730-825.
14. *Ibid.*, pp. 564-5.
15. Cf. Aiyangar (1942: LVII-LVIII).
16. This unequal treatment arose from various causes such as the localities where the authors lived, their familiarity with the holy places, and their predilections (Kane, *op. cit.*, p. 565).
17. See, *Sanskrit-English Dictionary*, Pt. I., P.K. Gode and C.G. Karve (1957), Poona; also *Sabdakalpadruma*.
18. See, *Buddhist Hybrid Sanskrit Grammar and Dictionary*, Vol. II, Franklin Edgerton (1970), Delhi.
19. Cf. Snellgrove (1959).
20. Cf. *Sabdakalpadruma*.
21. For an exhaustive list of Ganpati-kshetra, see Sharma (1975).
22. See Kane, *op. cit.*, pp. 730-825; also *Krtyakalpataru*.
23. See Snellgrove, *op. cit.*, X.2-5.
24. *Ibid.*
25. *Ibid.*
26. Cf. *Saraha's Dohakosa*; see, Buddhist Texts (Cassirer, 1954), pp. 230-1.
27. Cf. Kane, *op. cit.*, p. 628.

28. The description is based largely on the pattern of the temples of Kerala, as described by Iyer (1977: 17-8).
29. See Dhal (1977); also Kane, *op. cit.*, pp. 694-9.
30. See Saraswati (1975).
31. Cf. Saraswati (1977: 73-4)
32. See, for instance, Goswami and Morah (1975: 11-48).
33. See Kane, *op. cit.*, pp. 568-79.
34. *Ibid.*, pp. 604-12; also *Krtyakalpataru.*
35. *Ibid.*, pp. 574-75.
36. *Ibid.*, p. 655.
37. *Ibid.*, p. 697.
38. *Ibid.*, pp. 697-8.
39. See Saraswati (1975).
40. *Ibid.*
41. For details, see Bose (1961); Saraswati (1978); also Saraswati and Behura (1963).
42. See Saraswati (1977).
43. See Iyer, *op. cit.*, pp. 17-22.
44. *Ibid.*, pp. 42-58.
45. The *Pauranic tirthas* in south India are not much different from their counterparts in north India, but their number is small, and organization is predominantly on the pattern of temple towns—greatest importance is attached to temples rather than on the *kshetra.* For details of the *Pauranic* holy places in south India, see Thakur (1977); also Kane, *op. cit.*, pp. 730-825; *Krtyakalpataru;* Sharma, *op. cit.*
46. Cf. Bose (1963: 19).

REFERENCES

Aiyangar, K.V. Rangaswami (ed.) 1942. *Krtyakalpataru* (*Tirtha-vivechana-khanda*) of Bhatta Lakshmidhara. Baroda.

Bose, N.K. 1961. *Peasant Life in India: A Study in Indian Unity and Diversity.* Calcutta.

Bose, N.K. 1963. *Culture and Society in India.* Calcutta.

Dhal, U.N. 1977. Viraja-kshetra mahatmya of Brahmanda Purana: A survey, *Purana* 19 (2): 292-304.

Goswami, B.B. and S.G. Morab 1975. *Chamundesvari Temple in Mysore.* Calcutta.

Hazra, R.C. 1963. *Studies in the Upa-puranas.* Calcutta.

Iyer, S. Venkitasubramonia 1977. *Religion, Art and Culture.* Trivandrum.

Kane, P.V. 1953. *History of Dharmasastra*, vol. IV. Poona.

Kane, P.V. 1977. *Brahmanic Ritual Traditions: In the Crucible of Time.* Simla.

Kane, P.V. 1978. *Pottery-making Cultures and Indian Civilization.* Delhi.

Saraswati, Baidyanath 1975. *Kashi: Myth and Reality of a Classical Cultural Tradition.* Simla.

Saraswati, Baidyanath and Nab Kishore Behura 1963. *Pottery Techniques in Peasant India.* Calcutta.

Sharma, B.R. 1975. Ganapati and his most sacred places for pilgrimage in India, *Bhavan's Journal* 22 (3): 17-27.

Snellgrove, D.L. 1959. *The Hevajra Tantra: A Critical Study.* London.

Thakur, Umakant 1977. The holy places of south India as depicted in the Skanda Purana, *Purana* 19 (2): 305-20.

4

THE SACRED
The Proper Context of Poetry

HISTORIANS of literature examine poetry within a frame of historical perspectives: development of linguistic structure, diffusion of themes, depiction of historical events, historical personality of the composer, and the prevailing social conditions. The critic of literature determines the quality of poetic language: appropriateness of themes, aesthetic styles, imagery, composition, and the capacity to rouse human emotions. Both of these types of work are valuable for a student of anthropology, but none may fully serve his specific interest. For him the bare facts of history and the codex of empty stylistics are of little use unless they take him to the deeper dimensions of life and culture. The questions to which he would normally address himself are wide ranging. How truly does the poet interact with nature in his faith and dream? How effective is his poetry in the shaping of culture? How deep is his understanding of human attitude and temperament? How lasting is his impact upon the people? It follows, then, that the anthropologist seeks to understand poetry in its manifold fullness. But he himself cannot be the historian or the critic of poetry; he can only acquire the necessary background of the people's perception of poetry. In other words, his own task is to understand poetry as a cultural phenomenon.

NATURE, MAN AND POETRY

In all cultures poetry has been attributed to nature. It is often said, there is something divine about poetry: it is the god's gift; poets are born, not made. One might as well say: since poetry originates in the realm of the divine nature, in the realm of the sacred, the poet is closed to nature, closer to the sacred. In the *Atharva Veda* (10.8.32) there is a verse; *paśya devasya kavyam, na mamar na jeeryati*. Referring to nature, the *Rishi* says: "see the wisdom (*kavya*) of the god, he does not die, he grows not old". Here poetry has been identified with the cosmos. What came out as the revelation to the Vedic *Rishis* was in the form of poetry: hence, in a way, poetry precedes man.

But all cultures may not attach the same value to the role of nature in poetry, partly because different cultures have developed different views of man. The primitive cultures, for instance, recognize man as a part of society, which in turn is an integral part of nature and the cosmos.[1] The well-being of man is contingent upon his harmonious relationship with nature[2], which means harmony with the society. To bring a disorder in the society amounts to the disordering of nature, which means disordering oneself, destroying oneself. In the interest of his own existence man must, therefore, continually seek for balance. The balance can be maintained if the members of the society think[3] alike and act alike. Hence in the primitive societies all human activities are corporate actions. Poetry is also nobody's personal venture, because there is nothing personal there[4]: everyone is a poet, everyone is a singer. The entire corpus of primitive or folk poetry is, therefore, collective and anonymous. All pieces are of equal merit: there is nothing like good poetry and bad poetry.

In the classical cultures the perception of man is different. Here man is recognized as something apart from society and the cosmos.[5] One of the dominant views in the Hindu classical culture, for instance, is that man is essentially a spiritual being caught up in the bondage of *maya*, seeking his own personal salvation, independent of society—by renouncing the society, if necessary. Human activities are not to be shared equally by all: the act appropriate to a Brahman is not appropriate to a

Kshatriya, the act appropriate to a Kshatriya is not appropriate to a Vaishya, and the act appropriate to a Vaishya is not appropriate to a Shudra. The converse of this order is also true. Just as there are appropriate acts for different classes of men, so are there different proportions of *gunas* (strands of nature) reflecting in the four classes: the Brahmans reflect the dominance of *sattva* (goodness) *guna*, the Kshatriyas *rajas* (energy), the Shudras *tamas* (dullness), and the Vaishyas a mixture of *rajas* and *tamas*. Such an enigmatic conception of inequality in man's role and *gunas* would naturally make the situation in the Hindu society totally different from what has just been said about the primitive society. Here there is no inherent social compulsion for everyone to become a poet or a singer. Moreover, everyone cannot possess the vision of a poet, which rests so much on one's essentially personal and intrinsic quality determined by past *karma* and the grace of God. Hence there are different types of personalities: some are born genius, others mediocre. Thus, in contrast to the primitive or folk poetry, the classical poetry is personal. Even the Vedic poets, who followed the primitive mode of oral transmission have recorded the fact of their authorship.

PRIMITIVE, CLASSICAL AND MODERN POETRY

In the primitive societies, poetry is not isolated from other activities of life and hence there is no big difference between poetic language and the language of everyday life. A simple combination of words when spoken in a particular fashion—rhyme and rhythm—becomes poetry in a special sense. Poetry exists only as the words to music.[6] But howsoever insignificant the difference between the language of everyday life and poetic language may be, for a primitive man this difference is of very great importance. The mode of expression employed in interaction with nature has to be different from that employed in ordinary interaction with man. It is perhaps out of this consideration that in the primitive societies language is given a special form at ceremonial occasions. In the more developed form of primitive poetry, in what is called folk-poetry, the difference between the language of everyday life and poetic language may appear a little more conspicuous, but there also the purpose of difference remains the same, that is, to adopt a special mode of expression for ritualistic interaction with nature and the cosmos. The ritual utterances or the language used for healing and protection of life, for removal of evil spirits, and for the performance of rituals of all kinds has to be necessarily poetic, though at times it may not be meaningful in ordinary language. Another characteristic feature of the primitive poetry is its spontaneity and naturality. Poems are composed on the spot—dancing ground or a place of work—by the poet-singers. The themes of everyday life and culture, experiences of events, environments, and human beauty and deeply passionate love figure prominently in the primitive man's poetry. Because poems are composed on all occasions of life birth, marriage, death, economic pursuit and rituals—it may also be called "occasional poetry". The most striking feature of the primitive poetry, as indicated, is its impersonal character. No person is identified in poetry by his or her name. Among the Todas[7], for instance, when a song is addressed to a person, alive or dead, a buffalo's name is used in a vocative form instead of a personal name. All the identification that is provided consists of allusion to the patrilineal clan membership.

In the classical cultures the difference between the language of everyday life and poetic language is fundamental. The difference lies in the metrical composition of words and the rules of grammar (*chhanda shastra*). Poetic language is presented in a more complex format, and even when it is composed in prose form, it maintains a distinct character. In the *Yajur Veda*, for instance, the *mantras* composed in prose form have also been set in *chhandas*, so that they can be recited rhythmically. These *chhandas* are, of course, not the standard poetic *chhandas* used by the Vedic poets. Perhaps these prose *mantras* are the earliest example of what is now called prose-poetry. However, the purpose of making such conscious distinction between the poetic language of rituals and the language of everyday life remains the same as stated in the case of the primitive cultures. This is why in the Hindu classical culture, all poetry, in a real sense, is religious poetry. It has been said that the purpose of poetry (*kavya-prayojan*) is to achieve the Ultimate End (*moksha*) comprehended in the concept of *chaturvarga*[8] (*dharma*, *artha*, *kama* and *moksha*). The *kavya-mimamsa* of Rajasekhar[9]

7. The Shanta Durga temple of Goa

8. The Mangesh temple of Goa

9. The sacred gateway (*Gopura*) : the early 17th century superstructure of the Ramlingeshwara temple at Rameshvaram

mentions that, according to the ancient tradition, the Spirit of Poetry (*Kavya-Purusha*) was born of the goddess of learning (Saraswati) as a result of her long penance on the Himalayas, and was set by the Self-existent Being to promulgate the study of poetics in the three worlds. This sort of divination of poetry[10] in Sanskrit literature is found throughout its history. Hence not only ritualistic poetry and prayers, but in fact, all forms of poetry are immanently religious in character, and there is hardly anything in the Hindu classical literature which can be called truly "secular poetry". Even amatory poetry and erotic[11] songs are related to no human being but to gods. The earliest Indian poems, which give a passionate expression of the emotion of love, appear in the *Rig Veda* (X.95), in the form of a dialogue between Pururavas, a mortal, and Urvasi, a divine maiden, and again in the dialogue of Yama and Yami—the primeval twins. Later, Sanskrit love poetry, which was influenced by the science of erotics, continued depicting divine passion. The *Kumarasambhava* of Kalidas depicting the physical beauty of the goddess Parvati, and the *Gita-Govinda* of Jayadeva describing Radha's amorous sports with Krishna in erotic verses are the finest examples of religious poetry. All kinds of knowledge, even the knowledge of medicine and astronomy, revealed to the *Rishi*, have been transmitted in poetic form—the only form of language that can contain the sacred. Like the primitive poetry, the classical poetry may also be oral and occasional, but even then it assumes textual character and tends to be universal. But in contrast to the former, it consciously deals with abstract themes and is, hence, artificial.

In the "modern cultures" there is a total disregard for both the form and the purpose of poetry, which the primitive and the classical cultures have held in respect. In the opinion of traditional people, what goes under the name of "modern poetry" is an expression of total denial of all the traditional forms and ideas that take man into the realm of transcendence. "Modern" poetry has indeed desacralized itself inasmuch as it does not portray an exemplary model for humanities outside the historical situation of man. In breaking all conventions of poetic composition and themes it calls for "freedom" of man but apparently does not know what "freedom" means to man.

MYTH, HISTORY AND POETRY

Between the primitive poetry and the classical poetry there is a similarity in perceptivity, which to an anthropologist, appears more fundamental than their linguistic or structural differences: both perceive poetry as a phenomenon of the sacred. In this archaic approach poetry becomes essentially trans-historical.[12] The classical epics, for instance, describe events and personages, but they refer to mythical time instead of historical time, archetypes instead of historical personages. Nevertheless, for the archaic people they are *real*, only and precisely because they speak of what *really* happened and how the sacred became manifest.

This trans-historical character of epics precludes all empirical examinations: one cannot logically proceed to discover "historical truth" in them. One of my esteemed colleagues and a distinguished archaeologist Professor B.B. Lal, who has excavated the *Pauranic* sites of the *Ramayana* and the *Mahabharata*, told me that all the excavated sites associated with the *Ramayana* have a cultural affinity in so far as their earliest stratum of culture dates back to the same prehistoric time and produces the same type of material culture, which means a fair amount of correlation between the *Pauranic* tradition and the historical tradition,[13] but the earliest stratum of the *Mahabharata* is older than that of the *Ramayana*, which means the popular traditional theory of Ramavatar preceding Krishnavatar is false. My reply to him was that the archaeological finding has in no way falsified the traditional theory and that his interpretation is burdened with various types of difficulties. *First*, the very assumption that there can be a historical affinity between the places described in the epics and the places so identified in popular tradition is based on a false conception of the *Pauranic* places. The places identified as Ayodhya and Mathura are not the "original" places in a historical sense. They are the archetypes reproduced by ancient sages and seers—a fact so well-known to the students of the *Pauranic* studies. Ayodhya was reproduced not only at one place but at several places. Today, there is more than one Ayodhya, more than one Chitrakoota, more than one Lanka spread in different parts of India. In Kashi alone all these places, as also Mathura, Dwarka and Kurukshetra, are enshrined and every common man in the street knows that these are the archetypes and not the historical prototypes. The learned *Pauranicas* are aware of the doctrine of cosmic cycles (*yugas*) and the end of the world with a dissolution (*pralaya*). The Ramavatar has taken place in several different cosmic cycles (a complete cycle ends with a *pralaya*) and the places associated with him are washed away by the primordial floods—they are later reactualized by the great sage Markandeya.[14] *Second,* the fact that all the places associated with a particular epic have a prehistoric affinity shows how consistent and ancient the tradition of India is in reactualizing the sacred history. The logic that the historical chronological order does not tally with the traditional chronological order and hence the traditional theory is false stands on weak legs. There could be several possible explanations: It is likely that the *Mahabharata* being the later epic in popular memory was reactualized earlier than the *Ramayana* which belonged to the older age. In the *pitri-pujan* (ancestor worship), the last *pitri* is installed first and the other *pitris* follow in the reverse order of their historical time. In the like manner the traditional culture might have chosen a reverse order in the reactualization of the epics. This did not, of course, disturb the cultural consciousness of the people, because what is central to the understanding of the order between the *Treta yuga* and the *Dwapara yuga* is the "break"—the point of separation between the two *yugas*—and this has been scrupulously maintained in the space. *Third*, in the tradition of India time has neither beginning nor end (*anadi*, *ananta*) and space is supported by, and extended in, time.[15] Also, in the cyclic concept of *yuga* the question of early and late is totally irrelevant. If archaeological finding is to be taken seriously then it proves beyond doubt that in the reactualization of "initial" places the "original break" between the two *yugas* has been ingeniously demonstrated. *Fourth*, modern Ayodhya and Mathura are not only the exact reproduction of the "original" Ayodhya and Mathura, they exist in that same primordial time when Rama and Krishna performed there their *leelas:* for a *homo religious* the *leelas* are eternally performed in these places, and these can be seen at all times by

God's grace. In fact, it is this reproduction of both space and time that makes Ayodhya and Mathura sacred and *real.* But this reality is "sacred reality", different from historical reality.

Thus, it is only in the archaic consciousness that the epics describe *real* events and *real* personages.

THE SACRED

The proper context

Enough has been said to emphasize the point that the historical method is inapt in understanding poetry. Poetry must be examined in its own context. As stated, in the primitive and the classical cultures the proper context of poetry is the sacred. Indian historians and critics of literature have not so far studied this aspect of poetry. The German philosopher Martin Heidegger[16] has tried to explain the spiritual essence of poetry in his treatment of the poems of the nineteenth century poet Friedrich Holderlin. For him[17] true poetry is the vessel of the holy: "the inaugural naming of the gods and the essence of things". In his view what man works at and pursues does not touch the essence of his sojourn on this earth, does not reach the foundation of human existence which is fundamentally poetic. Interpreting Holderlin's poem "Full of merit, and yet poetically, dwells Man on this earth", he[18] says: to dwell poetically means to stand in the presence of the gods and to be involved in the proximity of the essence of things. Heidegger[19] holds that the great mission which poetry from the beginning has had is the establishment of being by means of the word—establishment not only in the sense of free act of giving but in the sense of the firm basing of human existence on its foundation. This act of establishment in his[20] view is subject to a two-fold control:

> The writing of poetry is the fundamental naming of gods. But the poetic words only acquire its power of naming, when gods themselves bring us to language. . . . The establishment of being is bound to the signs of gods. And at the same time the poetic word is only the interpretation of the voice of the people. . . . In this way

> the essence of the poetry is joined on the laws of the signs of gods and of the voice of the people, laws which tend towards and away from each other. The poet himself stands between the former—gods, and the latter—the people. He is one who has been cast out—out into that between, between gods and men.

Several centuries before Heidegger, Plato had spoken of poets as being filled with god and had placed them on the same footing as the oracular bards or soothsayers.[21] In the tradition of India, poetry has always remained a pursuit in divinity. The ancient poet-philosopher and the medieval poet-saint of India have been regarded as *avatari-purusha* (an incarnate being). What was revealed to them came in the form of poetry and when they responded to gods, the same was also in the form of poetry: the *Ramayana* was revealed to the illiterate Valmiki, and similarly, the medieval illiterate saints communicated with gods in the language of poetry. For them, using Holderlin's expression, to "dwell poetically" means to dwell religiously.

Unless we conceive this essence of poetry we cannot possibly answer why in a certain society there is incompatibility between the "poetic value" and the "secular value": How is it that the poets acquire an impersonal character in Hindu society which scrupulously maintains personal diacritical marks in all contexts of secular life? Most ancient Indian poets did not record their authorship and the medieval poet-saints composed poetry mostly in the name of their guru. The answer to this question lies not in history but in 'ethno-philosophy'—the people's perception of reality.

To illustrate, let us take the example of Kabirian poetry. When the followers of Kabir, a medievel poet-saint, compose poetry in the name of their Kabir-guru they have the satisfaction of performing *dharma* (meritorious duty). In support of their belief what they explain runs something like this: "The writing of poetry is a religious pursuit. Some compose poems; others who have no talents to do so transcribe the Kabirian poem—making several copies—for the use of fellow-religionists. By writing poems in the name of their guru they are adding to the guru's 'power' (*guru ka pratapa badhana*, as they call it) and in this way they serve their guru better, come to him closer, and earn merit. They have already surrendered themselves to their guru: nothing remains of their own. Their entire existence lies on *guru-pratapa*, and so what they compose is, in reality, the composition of their guru." To present their explanation in a more sophisticated manner: when the followers of a poet-guru compose poems in the name of their guru they speak the words of the guru and not their own—"their own personality is totally switched off so that they are representatives absolutely and completely".[22] By doing so they reactualize their guru, earn the merit of imitating an exemplary model.

Thus, from the people's point of view, the poems composed by the followers of a poet-saint are *really* the poems of that poet-guru. This shows that the proper context of poetry is the sacred, and not personal history.

Similarly, the proper context of poetry is not language. To put it differently: poetry cannot be properly understood in terms of language. This might seem an over-bold proposition, but nevertheless it is true. In all cultures poetry came earlier than the written prose. Heidegger[23] has rightly stated:

> Poetry never takes language as a raw material ready to hand, rather it is poetry which first makes language possible. Poetry is the primitive language of a historical people. Therefore, in just the reverse manner, the essence of language must be understood through the essence of poetry.

From the point of view of a literary critic a certain unintelligible variety of poetry, for instance, the *ulatabansi* of Kabirian poetry and the *sandhya bhasa* of the Chariyageeti may be unimportant and meaningless, but it has indeed and intrinsic positive value for the poet as also for the people. It has been repeatedly emphasized in the tradition of India that the manifest human language (*vaikhari*) is inadequate to communicate the *reality*. Hence, whenever a poet wants to speak of that reality and fails to do so through the ordinary language he imitates the primordial language which is unintelligible and meaningless in the language of everyday life. The language used in chants, as stated, is also unintelligible but efficacious and hence *real* for the people. Thus the real meaning of poetry lies not in its language but in the deeper faiths of man.

In conclusion, it might be said: the proper context of poetry is the sacred. Its supreme function is to kindle the faiths and hopes in mankind. The religious poetry performs this function admirably, and hence has a lasting impact upon the people. This is very widely reflected in the primitive cultures as also in the classical Hindu traditions of poetry.

NOTES

1. See Kitagawa (1967: 39-65).
2. In the Zuni world-view, for instance, there is a harmonious identification of God, nature, and man in one enduring recurrent system. Here the "duty of man is the performance of those collective rituals that maintain a perpetual and unchanging harmonious oneness of God, man, and nature. The attitude is one of doing one's part in a persistent system." (Redfield 1953: 99).
3. Redfield (*Ibid.*, p. 89) has pointed out that among the Andamanese what one man thinks is not too different from what most of them think.
4. In primitive jurisprudence the clan is the only legal person, the one body and entity. "The unit is not the individual, but the kin. The individual is but part of the kin", are the words of Mr. Sidney Hartland. Cf. Malinowski (1947: 48).
5. "Man comes out from the unity of the universe within which he is oriented now as something separate from nature and comes to confront nature as something with physical qualities only, upon which he may work his will". (Redfield *op. cit.*, p. 108.)
6. Herskovits (1960: 433).
7. Emeneau (1959: 113).
8. "The *caturvarga* and the other material objects of poetry are mentioned in almost unbroken tradition; but with the elaboration of a full-fledged scheme poetics in connection with the suggestion of *Rasa*, the purpose of poetry was brought into a level with the ultimate theory about its nature; and poetry was supposed to create a peculiar mood of aesthetic pleasure, conveyed generally by the philosophic term *ananda*. Jagannath (the famous poet and the author of the celebrated *Bhamini-vilasa*) completes the idea by defining it as a disinterested or dissociated (*alaukika*) pleasure (divine pleasure), which depends upon a taste formed by repeated representation of beautiful objects, and which can be enjoyed by a man initiated into the poetic mysteries." (De 1960: 40-1).

9. *Ibid.*, pp. 35, 292, 293.
10. Every *sukta* of the Vedic poetry has been assigned a Devata (God), Rishi (the poet-sage), *Chhanda* and *Swara*.
11. "Sanskrit love-poetry gives us a miniature picture of love, not in its simplicities but in the niceties, not in its large and direct exaltations but in its moments and moods of delicate subtlety. Sanskrit poetry, much less its love poetry, with its implications and reticences, is never simple and untutored in the sense in which these terms can be applied to modern poetry: It is never undisciplined nor meant for indisciplined enjoyment. . . . The sentiment is more often artistic than personal. This is in perfect accordance with the Sanskrit poetic theory of impersonalized enjoyment, which would rule out personal passion and permit the theme , not of a particular woman, . . . but of women as such. . . . It is true that the particular woman is always there behind the universalised woman, and inspires the emotional earnestness and vivid imagery; but in the refined and idealised expression there is little scope for personal emotion.

    "The science of Erotics had indeed a profound influence on the theory and practice of the poetry . . . although we must guard against the error of assuming that the classical erotic poetry is in the nature of pornography." (De 1969: 15-6, 20).

    For the Vaishnava erotic songs, see Sinha (1961, 1966).
12. For an excellent account of mythicization of historical personages in heroic poetry, see Eliade (1954: 37-42).
13. This tendency towards establishing a link between the *Pauranic* and the historical tradition was found among the nineteenth century scholars. Bankim Chandra Chatterjee wanted to establish the historicity of the *Mahabharata*. In the recent years Professors H.D. Sankalia, D.C. Sircar, and several other historians figured prominently in a public debate on the question of historicity of the *Ramayana* and the *Mahabharata*. S.C. De (1976) has published a well-documented book on the historicity of the *Ramayana*. Those who have tried to establish the historicity of the epics are sadly mistaken in their understanding of its purpose. The purpose of the epic is not to retain or transmit the historical persons and events but to transmit the message (social and divine) among the people as lesson of life.
14. The great sage Markandeya is believed to be the only one who has seen the *pralaya* and who is born in another *yuga* to tell the tale of the previous era. From him the other *Rishis* learn about what really happened in the past, and accordingly the places associated with Rama or Krishna are reactualized.
15. Panikkar (1967: 65-6).
16. See Heidegger (1949: 293-315) on Holderlin and the Essence of poetry.
17. *Ibid.*, p. 307.

18. *Ibid.*, p. 306.
19. *Ibid.*, p. 305.
20. *Ibid.*, p. 312.
21. Apology, 22; cf. on the Greek "man of words", Murray, *The rise of the Greek Epics*, 118: "The ancient 'man of words' was not exactly a story-teller, not exactly a chronicler, not exactly a magician. He was all these, and something more." Cf. Van der Leeuw (1938: 226).
22. *Ibid.*, 21. 1, p. 222.
23. Heidegger, *op. cit.*, p. 307.

REFERENCES

De, S.C. 1976. *Historicity of Ramayana and the Indo-Aryan Society in India and Ceylon*. Delhi.

De, Sushil Kumar 1960. *History of Sanskrit Poetics*, vol. II. Calcutta.

De, Sushil Kumar 1969. *Ancient Indian Erotics and Erotic Literature*. Calcutta.

Eliade, Mircea 1954. *The Myth of the Eternal Return*. New York.

Emeneau, M.B. 1959. Oral poets of south India—the Todas. In Milton Singer (ed.) *Traditional India: Structure and Change*. Philadelphia.

Heidegger, Martin 1949. *Existence and Being*. London.

Herskovits, Meliville J. 1960. *Man and His Works*. New York.

Kitagawa, Joseph M. 1967. Primitive, classical and modern religions: a perspective on understanding the history of religion. In Joseph M. Kitagawa *et al* (ed.) *The History of Religions: Essays in Divinity*, vol. I. Chicago.

Malinowski, Bronislaw 1947. *Crime and Custom in Savage Society*. London.

Panikkar, Raimundo 1976. Time and history in the tradition of India: kala and karma. In *Culture and Time*. UNESCO, Paris.

Redfield, Robert 1953. *The Primitive World and Its Transformations*. New York.

Sinha, Surajit 1961. A note on the concept of sexual union for spiritual quest among the Vaisnava preachers in the Bhumij belt of Purulia and Singhbhum, *The Eastern Anthropologist* 14 (2), 194-6.

Sinha, Surajit 1966. Vaisnava influence on a tribal culture. In Milton Singer (ed.) *Krishna: Myth, Rites and Attitudes*. Honolulu.

Van der Leeuw, G. 1938. *Religion in Essence and Manifestation: A Study in Phenomenology*. London.

5

UNDERSTANDING SACRED TRADITIONS
An Essay on the Structure and Functions of Religion

THE ANTHROPOLOGICAL works on religion fall under two broad categories: one constituting the early classical works pertaining to the origin and evolution of religion, as rendered by Spencer, Tylor, Frazer, Marett and Durkheim, and the other, constituting the subsequent analytic descriptive studies of social functions of religion, as suggested by Malinowski, Radcliffe-Brown and others. The ideas and interpretations which most of these path-finders have generated in religious research were based primarily upon the data from what are called the primitive peoples. And because we continue to follow them faithfully, both in approach and in interpretations, the conceptual universe of our modern anthropological writings and research in sophisticated religions like Buddhism and Hinduism has remained essentially the same as that of the early studies of the primitive belief system. What is required is to develop a new perspective which may help our understanding of the real spectrum of religion in its elementary form as also in its most developed form. It is only then that we can make a viable generalisation of the religious phenomena, whether we examine them as anthropologists or as philosophers and phenomenologists.

The general anthropological assumption is that all religious beliefs are woven round a "fear complex" which is perpetually fed by man's limitations in controlling the cause of his life and of his environment. That there is a "power" higher than man which guides the destiny of all living beings is a belief augmented by this experience, and that such belief eventually lies at the root of all kinds of rituals of propitiation or conciliation of that "power" which occasionally manifests itself at places and in persons and objects. That certain men attain the knowledge of transcendence which enables them to communicate with that "power", and it is from the cultivation and transmission of the knowledge of that "power" that grows a body of "specialists". That at the time of human crisis and need these "specialists" act as an intermediary between the lay-man and the superhuman being, and that the "true" way of life is, therefore, believed to be known only to them. This entitles them to prescribe and perform the rituals and to lay the code of conduct known as morality. Their interpretation of the universe is what we call philosophy. Finally, individuals or communities that articulate with the "specialists" take and adapt the latter's prescriptions in various cultural forms, and thus become the carrier of a sacred tradition known as "religion".

THE STRUCTURE OF RELIGION

From all that has been said above, it comes out that the structure of religion is a set of relationship between three components: (i) the belief in superhuman beings, (ii) the "specialists" who create such belief, and (iii) the laity who receive it in various forms. The belief in superhuman beings is expressed in terms of their form, functions, and relationship with human beings. In other words, there is a conception of the existence of a phenomenon which is autonomous and independent of the natural order and yet inextricably linked with the human world. That phenomenon is called the "sacred" as something qualitatively different from the natural phenomenon called the "secular". Although the sacred relates to a transnatural order—a wholly different kind of reality—it is knowable and approachable. Of all the creatures on the earth man alone can acquire the knowledge of that transcendence. It is also a compelling necessity that man must seek, in his own interest, the knowledge of the "sacred". Since the "sacred" affects the course of human life, its power must be harnessed or it may be approached amicably. Perhaps there is or there is not a permanent solution of human crisis—freedom from the bondage of "suffering" in a collective sense. But individually, there are ways to "free" oneself permanently. The solution lies in maintaining a harmonious relationship with the "sacred", and hence all religious persons—the seekers of this solution—are located at different points of harmony. The point where the finest and the purest relationship can be established is the point of merger : total and complete. The merger is of the two sets of orders: two beings, the "sacred" and the "secular", the knower and the known. The implication is that these two sets of order can possibly be made up into one continuum.

The "sacred" manifests itself at places, in persons and objects, and hence there is an opportunity at the temporal level to communicate and to establish relationship with the "sacred". The way through which this relationship is established is called "ritual", and because it performs a humanistic function, ritual is the core component of all religions. It is the actualization of the belief in supernatural world. Since it deals with non-human phenomena which cannot be explained in terms of ordinary human language, it has to follow necessarily symbolic code. For the same reason it is also an archetypal behaviour. The hypothesis, therefore, is that greater the complexity of ritual the more complex will be the structure of a religion. The converse is also true, that is, simpler the ritual the more elementary will be the form of religion.

The knowledge which determines ritual is revealed to extraordinary persons. It may also be gained through human efforts in an extraordinary state of mind. The human ways of acquiring such knowledge are esoteric, but there are definite guidelines. In fact, there is what might be called the craft of spirituality. Anthropologists of religion have, however, made little contribution to the understanding of this craft, especially of the more complex and developed variety. For instance, anthropological researches have not so far attempted to answer a number of questions: What are the contents of transcendental knowledge? How is this knowledge cultivated, transmitted and perpetuated? What special qualifications regarding body and mind or social background are needed for achieving this knowledge? How are the "specialists" in transcendental knowledge motivated? How do they transcend the normal inclinations? And, what makes them qualitatively different from the ordinary human beings? One might say that these are not the proper subject matter of anthropology, and their answers may profitably be sought in the Yoga-Tantra. But the modern anthropologists working on complex religions can hardly justify this statement. In fact, they cannot afford to leave out these questions unanswered. After all, transcendence is the construction of the human mind, and there are groups of men devoted exclusively to the cultivation of this idea. The pursuit of transcendence is not only an exploration of human mind—the field of psychologists—but basically a human craft of knowing the "ultimate concern" of man and of all living beings. At the empirical level, one can see that it is a full-time occupation, like any other human occupation. Indeed, the cultivation of excellence in religion is as absorbing a profession as any other, say music or painting. Those who are directly and constructively involved in the pursuits of transcendental knowledge, such as the *Yogis* form an in-group, renounce the ordinary social life and behave in a manner different from the other groups of men. So far as the modes of transmission of knowledge are concerned, the same form a distinct cultural category. In any case, they are linchpin of the religious belief system and guide our social behaviour, and hence we must know who they are, what they are, and how they operate the tradition of transcendence.

One thing which we do not know adequately is the thought processes involved in the origination of spiritual belief: Whether the form of the belief conceived at the "source" is transmitted to the laity wholesale or in parts, and to what extent it changes in between its original source and the societal ground where it is manifest. These points have a direct bearing upon our conception of belief as they are the products of human thought processes. To illustrate their relevance, let us take the example of belief in God. I should like to posit the whole processes in this way: The idea of God was first conceived by a "specialist" in transcendental knowledge, say by a Yogi, through the mystic way of revelation. Having thus obtained, the Yogi realised that what he has conceived or perceived cannot be communicated to others through the medium of human language. In Hindu philosophic tradition it has been said that the Brahmajnani (the one who has attained the knowledge of Brahma, the Absolute) becomes speechless, and hence when he is asked whether the Brahma that he has conceived of is like this or like that, in terms of concrete mundane objects, he says *neti, neti* "not this, not this". The Yogi admits that although the "thing" that he has conceived is *avachya* (indescribable) he can, however, say that "It is all-powerful". This means, he communicates, through the linguistic channel, that God is omnipotent. But what he says is only a part of his 'personal' conception of God. From him this partial idea of God passes on to the laity through another kind of lesser "specialists", namely, the pandits and the priests, which means further partialization of the idea of God by another agency. In fact the result of this partialization is that even the original partial idea of God, conceived by the Yogi, does not reach the common people—the non-specialists—intact or in its "true" original form. For instance, the pandits of Kashi perpetuate a belief that the *linga* of Visheshwara in Kashi is omnipotent and hence worthy of propitiation. The laymen or the pilgrims who flock round the Visheshwara temple have no knowledge of the exact nature of the omnipotency of God, or as the one conceived by the Yogi or, in most cases, even by the pandits. But what they believe in is the omnipotency of the *linga* of Visheshwara which (they have been told by the priests), has the power to fulfil all their mundane desires. Thus, the common people's belief in God, does not remain the same, either in quantity or in quality, as was originally conceived by the Yogi.

Similarly, each belief which passes on from one person to another carries in it some personal elements in each case and thus in course of this processes it loses its original form. Therefore, all religious beliefs of the common people are in a degenerated and incomplete form of what actually the "specialists" might have in their store of esoteric knowledge.

The study of belief as an integral part of a religious system will remain incomplete and inconclusive if it examines only the common people's belief at the secondary stage of the thought process, without taking into account the role of "specialists" as a generating force behind it.

Thus, the belief in the "sacred", the creator of the belief, and the believer are the three basic constituents of all religions. These are placed in an ordered relationship, where the "sacred" is considered in some religions as the supreme power upon which depends the well-being of man and all creatures, and in some others as the primeval being to be known and to be merged with: becoming one with it. This being is conceived differently in different religions, and hence there are various concepts of gods and spirits. But all religions consider "it" as *real* and functional, as "something" which gives and takes away life, and creates, destroys and/or recreates the perceptible world. The "specialist" who cultivates this belief occupies a privileged position in all religions, in all societies, precisely because he explains the sacred, performs rituals and acts as an intermediary. In the category of "believers" there may also be some persons who are negatively related to the idea of supernatural, in so far as they deny its existence.

A religion continues in existence as an ordered arrangement of the three aforesaid components, though the idea of the "sacred", the knowledge of the "specialists" and the personnel who are involved in it as specialists or the laity change from time to time. The religion of a people changes only in the sense of its organizational character, that is, changes brought about the natural course of development in personal thought process or by conversion. And it is also the organizational content that differentiates the religions of the world from one another. But any change in the ordering of the three basic components will eventually bring a disastrous discontinuity in the structure of religion, as has happened in modern technological society.

FUNCTIONS OF RELIGION

In the anthropological study of religion what is thought

important is the social function of religion, that is, its effect in maintaining a harmonious social order. This view also presupposes the disharmonious role of religion. For instances, all proselytizing religions create a situation in which the believers and the non-believers remain in constant conflict and tension. Even within a religion, all faithful religious persons may often be subject to ideological conflicts. There are several instances of the earnest devotees undergoing self-torture purely as a matter of choice. Mira Bai, the celebrated devotee of Sri Krishna, for instance, had to choose between her conjugal love and the love to God. She, of course, made a choice for the latter and eventually took a draught of poison. Since religion occupies the most sensitive area of human mind, it can be used effectively for both creative and destructive purposes. But the most important function is, of course, to offer peace-making and solidarious elements to both man and society. This may be further illustrated for the sake of clarity.

Physical presence of the sacred

As stated, the "sacred" manifests itself at places, in persons, and in objects. In the primitive belief system the world is densely populated with supernatural beings. They exist almost everywhere in nature—in trees, forests, fields, rivers, mountains, plants and animals. The spirits are of two kinds: the one that can do much harm and the other that can do much good. There may also be a spirit in which both the malevolent and the benevolent characters combine. However, the presence of the spirits is not only natural but also necessary. Their pleasure is sought to aid all affairs of man—the life-long search for food, shelter, progeny, and protection from both human and non-human enemies.

The concept of the supernatural being as the giver of reward and punishment implies that religion must have an ethical content and that it must play a vital role in maintaining social order. There are societies where most political and social decisions are taken by the personified supernatural beings. The best example of this can be cited of the Kinner society. The Kinners of Himachal Pradesh propitiate a large number of ruling deities called Devi-Devata. The Devi-Devatas

10. The sacred ghats of Varanasi on the Ganga : general view from Dashashwamedh to Panchaganga

11. The Varanasi ghats : Narada ghat, Raja ghat

are hierarchically arranged, and each one of them rules a specific territory like a benevolent monarch. The Devi Chandika is the chief ruler of the whole of Kinnaur. Her subordinate Devi-Devatas follow the traditional politico-administrative jurisdiction, and hence each of the territorial subdivisions, like *khund*, *ghori*, *gaon* (village) and *kim* (house) has a presiding deity. The Devi-Devatas are concerned about the well-being of the people. Among their multifarious functions are included the roles to solve inter-personal disputes of all kinds, to determine social norms regarding commensality and marriage, and to keep the evil spirits and ghosts away from human life and habitation. It is believed that the village deity keeps a watch on every action and occurence in the village, and accordingly rewards or punishes a person. It functions as a doctor, a judge, a social-worker, a match-maker, a fortune-teller or a fortune-maker, and a master of all trades. To maintain control over the situation and for smooth functioning of social life the Kinner deities periodically visit the places which fall under their jurisdiction. When a superior deity tours the area of the subordinate deities it receives from the latter all the care and attention which an inspecting officer receives from his subordinates. Similarly, when a subordinate deity visits the superior deity for consultation, advice and help, the ceremonial protocol is reciprocated. The villagers accord a warm send-off to the deity when it goes on tour, and a hearty welcome on its return. The deity addresses the general assembly of the village and conveys his views and orders. Like a king the village deity appoints a team of servants, usually once in three years, to help it in the affairs of administration. Of these, the two most important ones are the Groksha and the Matha. The former is a person in whom the deity takes possession and through whom it converses with the people; the latter is the mediator who conveys the people's requests to the deity through the Groksha and also tells back the people the deity's response to their requests, complaints and problems. It may be stated that in this process the personality of the Groksha is totally switched off so long as he is possessed by the deity and operates and exercises effective control over the people.

In Brahmanic Hinduism the places where the "sacred"

presents itself are called the *tirthas*, and the persons in whom it takes possession are called the holymen—the *sannyasis*, the *vairagis*, the *mahatmas*, and the like. The temples are the abodes of gods and goddesses. There is also the concept of *Avatar*—the incarnation of God Vishnu. The cow is a holy animal, and there are also birds and trees which possess spiritual quality. These manifestations of the "sacred" have important functions in the social and cultural life of the people. The holy places, for instance, help the patterning of cultures, integrate a wide variety of cultures, cultivate excellence, and preserve ideal types. The ascetics are like the pole-star; they symbolize the highest and steadiest ideas which the householders must try to attain. And God himself incarnates on the earth whenever there is a serious decay of righteousness.

In the Mahayana Buddhism, the Dalai Lama, the sKushak or the Rimpoche is the incarnation of the "sacred". Their presence in the society is treated as the presence of the "sacred" itself. In Christianity and Islam the Messiah and the prophet are treated as the persons in direct contact with the "sacred". There are oracles, soothsayers, witches and sorcerers who possess spiritual power, of course, of a lower kind.

What comes out from these allusions are: (a) that all religions demonstrate the physical presence of spirituality; (b) that such demonstration is necessary for fostering the belief they propagate; (c) that spiritual presence must be efficacious in maintaining a system of sentiments, in regulating human feelings; (d) that it must display 'power' for effective functioning of the society; and (e) that it must be institutionalized to keep the system alive and active.

Ritual

As stated, ritual is the core component of all religions. The rules governing ritual behaviour are transmitted orally or through the liturgical texts of a formally organized religion. Through ritual action flows the well-being not only of the performer but also of the performing society. The social world is thought to be protected by ritual. Hence, ritual is, by definition, an obligatory social behaviour prescribed for occasions that have reference to belief system. It is also a symbolic act that holds the ritual participants together as a community of belief and community of action. Ritual provides a system of meaning which validates both the social world and the cosmic world. Sharing of ritual experiences generates a deeper feeling, a truly human bond—intimate and personal. As a culturally patterned behaviour, firmly rooted in tradition, ritual is a subject of heuristic importance.

The study of ritual, so far attempted in Indian anthropology, is confined to the description and analysis of its structural form and symbols. The socio-cultural functions of ritual have been rarely studied. The fact that ritual is essentially a social behaviour and that it contributes significantly to the maintenance of a social order can hardly be disputed. In Brahmanic tradition, no ritual is obligatory for an asocial *sannyasi*—an ascetic who has renounced the society—while it is incumbent on every member of the society to perform the obligatory ritual. In view of such indigenous exegetic considerations, most anthropologists would refuse to limit the use of the term "ritual" to religious situations only. The term "religious ritual" is sometimes used for ritual behaviour specifically oriented towards sacred phenomena as against those ritual actions which are performed on purely secular occasions. Several different kinds of human affairs are thus covered within the broad spectrum of ritual.

A wide variety of questions from this point of view has remained unanswered in anthropological literatures on ritual: What adaptive functions does ritual serve? What makes it an obligatory social behaviour? What makes it a core component of culture and structure? How does it help maintain a unity of purposes in the diversities of social actions? How does it help establish relationship between individuals and groups, sometimes outside structure? What are the minimum ritual requirements of a society? What are the areas of social interaction where ritual is essential? What are the diacritical marks of life-affirming and life-negating, or auspicious and inauspicious rituals? How is the exegetic meaning of ritual determined, and how does it change? How do ritual traits serve as markers of culture? Does a ritual complex form a regional cultural pattern across religion, language and ethnicity?

Following are the humanistic functions of ritual.

Ritual : a means of socialization

In all societies, ritual is performed on different occasions of the life-cycles of individuals. In Brahmanic society, for instance, what goes under the rubric of *samskara* is a codex of life-cycle ritual requirements incumbent on every member of the society. These rituals are of two classes: one consisting of rites associated with bodily *samskaras*, from conception to cremation, and the other relating to the daily and seasonal sacrifices. However, at the functional level, no such distinction can be made, for both these classes aim at the socialization of individuals.

Ritual : a means of social control

Ritual legitimizes social life and maintains social order. It is linked with the eschatological belief regarding the rewards and punishments. The greatest elaboration of ritual takes place in the purificatory rites prescribed for the atonement of guilt. Ritual is an integral part of a normative system. The social order, in traditional societies, is based upon the supernatural order which in turn thrives on the proper performance of ritual. To bring any disorder in the society amounts to the disordering of the spiritual order, which means disordering oneself, destroying oneself. In the same manner, by maintaining the ritual order one maintains both the social order and the spiritual order. The ritual is an efficacious means of controlling social life.

Ritual : a means of acquiring merit and status

Merit flows from ritual. Different rites are prescribed for different occasions, for different purposes. The power of ritual gets manifest only when it is performed in the true spirit. Ritual benefits not only the performer but also the performing society, and even the strangers around the place of performance. Hence, by performing ritual one gets both spiritual merit and social eminence. In traditional societies, prestige is gained by the performance of ritual rather than the mere possession of wealth. Man's social status is traditionally measured by the number of rituals performed. In a sense, ritual is a quest for merit and status.

Ritual : a mode of identification

In all societies, the initiation rite is essential for every individual to become a fullfledged member. There are many other rites of identification. The central purpose of ritual mutilation is to modify the social position or personality of the individual. The rite of circumcision, perforation of earlobe or nose, tatooing, and such other practices are the marks of identification. Ritual mode of kinship-identification is commonly employed at the time of initiation, marriage and death. All types of kinship—both real and fictitious—are regulated through the ritual process.

Ritual : a means of spiritual advancement

In all universal religions, elaborate ritual is prescribed for the spiritual advancement of human beings. The most intricate form of ritual, known as *Tantra* in Brahmanic and Buddhist cultures, is meant for attaining the spiritual height. The rites of prayer, pilgrimage and worship in Islam and Christianity are also directed to this end. Esoteric rites for acquiring spiritual power are widely prevalent in traditional societies.

Ritual : a mode of nonverbal communication

Ritual is interpreted through a complex symbolic code. It has both esoteric and exoteric meanings. Ritual action, objects, words, gestures, and ritual space, used in nonverbal communication with the invisible powers, often follow an archetypal pattern.

Ritual : a mode of social interaction

Performances of ritual are essential on occasions of establishing or breaking relationship such as on initiation, friendship, marriage, divorce and death. Ritual is performed also in social prestations. It is a collective action when performed for collective ends. Ritual provides special occasions for social interaction such as congregational prayer, pilgrimage, fairs and festivals. It provides diacritical marks of social inequality, as in the Varna-based society, which means it controls social interaction. But, in another context, as on the occasions of fairs, festivals and pilgrimage, it also removes social inequality temporarily. The equalitarian ideology—*homo aequalis*—can be transmitted more effectively through the ritual code.

Ritual : a mode of cultivation of excellence

In all traditional societies—both literate and primitive—music, dance, drama and other fine arts and crafts are cultivated invariably through the ritual mode. In the Brahmanic tradition, man's desire of enjoying beauty and his sense of aesthetics are amply fulfilled in ritual performances. This is truly reflected in the selection of ritual objects and motifs, in the style of ritual action or performance, in the choice of ritual space of time and season, and such other considerations as may make ritual pleasing and absorbing. No Brahmanic ritual is devoid of aesthetic value.

Ritual : a mode of therapy

The institution of witchcraft and sorcery is well-developed in traditional societies. Esoteric rites are prescribed for causing and curing sickness. Ritual cure or faith healing is common also in universal religions. Elaborate ritual is prescribed in Brahmanic scriptures for rejuvenation and curing sickness caused by supernatural phenomena. Some ritual actions such as Yogic exercises, ritual food and fast, taboos, and the daily routine of ritual performances are in fact the golden rules of health care.

Ritual : a means of occupation

Ritual specialists are found in all societies. In the Brahmanic society, which has developed a highly complex ritual system, there are several different kinds of ritual specialists whose principal source of livelihood is the ritual performance for others. In all societies, priests enjoy certain privileges and economic benefits. At no other place can one see ritual a lucrative occupation as in Hindu places of pilgrimage. Also, ritual is associated with all kinds of occupation such as hunting, fishing, agriculture, and industrial arts and crafts.

Ritual : a way of life
A *homo religiosus* lives in the ritually constructed world. For him there is no other world, no other way of life. Elaborate rituals are prescribed for daily routine and annual ceremonies and festivities. Ritual makes life absorbing, pleasing and purposeful. Such indigenous interpretation of the functions of ritual is perspicuous at the exegetic level.

Besides these humanistic social functions, one of the most critical aspects of ritual is its cosmological function. The Vedic ritual, for instance, is based on a much wider principle. From the sacrifice (*Yajna*) have originated all beings. Sacrifice is the ruler of gods; it is the ultimate principle of existence; it preserves the universe; it is the most ineffable power. The Atharva Veda mentions its origin as follows:

1. Through sacrifice gods sacrificed to the Sacrifice.
   Those were the first established rites.
   Their greatness enhanced, they ascended to heaven where dwell the ancient gods who must needs be appeased.
2. Thus originated sacrifice; it manifested itself.
   It came to birth and then increased.
   It became the Lord and the ruler of gods.
   May sacrifice bestow upon us some treasure.

(*AV VII, 5*)

In the post-Vedic development, sacrifice lost its original meaning and significance. It began to be viewed under a more personalistic perspective as a ritual by which man may attain the fulfilment of human secular desires—material riches, offspring, power, triumph and the like.

RELIGION : A PERSONAL QUEST

Notwithstanding its humanistic social functions, religion is essentially a personal quest. Religious experiences are immanently personal: often incommunicable, deeply, absorbing and satisfying. For a *homo religious*, religiosus life is the only authentic existence and his experiences are the only realities.

He is not bothered by someone interpreting his act as irrational or in terms of sacred and profane. In his search for Truth, his life is elevated to an unrestricted plain and he is no longer limited by social considerations—in some cases he formally renounces the "social world".

Thus, in the ultimate analysis, religious life inevitably negates social life, destroys cultural boundaries, and liberates every person individually. This may appear as a far-fetched conclusion to those who are limited by empirical analysis of the external forms and functions of religion. But those who care to explore the more intrinsic experiences of religious persons may find some truth in this trans-anthropological assumption.

PART TWO

6

STUDYING THE SACRED COMPLEX IN KASHI

FOLLOWING the publication of Vidyarthi's monumental work, *The Sacred Complex in Hindu Gaya* (1961), some of his students became interested in the study of sacred centres in India. Some places of pilgrimage (*tirthas*) were studied directly under his guidance, and it came out that his findings have a wider applicability. In the *tirthas* of ancient origin a uniform cultural pattern is grounded on the canons of *Smritis* and *Puranas*. Gaya being one of the *Pauranic tirthas* has acquired an all-India character. And it is in this context of understanding a wider cultural tradition that Vidyarthi's contribution to Indian anthropology in general and the study of Indian sacred tradition in particular is both original and fundamental. But, at any rate, in such a vast field of knowledge his work was only of exploratory nature. He was concerned mainly with the organization of the Gayawalas—a priestly community—and was obviously influenced by Robert Redfield, Milton Singer and McKim Marriott, in his approach to the understanding of this cultural phenomenon. Nevertheless, he examined the structure of the sacred anew and described it as a sacred complex composed of three elements—(1) sacred geography, (2) sacred performances, and (3) sacred specialists. While there could be a general agreement on this trichotomic compound of the sacred, many questions regarding its nature and organization have remained unanswered in his work.

And hence, there is a need to re-examine the sacred complex from a new perspective.

PERSPECTIVE

After going round the various parts of India and doing continuous fieldwork in Kashi for more than five years I was left with no doubt that Kashi is an extraordinary city of India which personifies the totality of Indian cultural traditions. Not that it was my discovery. Almost innumerable scholars have sung the saga of this great "traditional city", also described as the "microcosm of Hinduism". But what came to me most clearly was that Kashi could not be bound to such a narrow limit of time, or to a particular sect and religion, or to a single strand of culture. In other words, to me, Kashi is more than a "traditional city", more than a "sacred city", more than the "microcosm of Hinduism", and, in fact, than all those epithets which have so far been attributed to this most ancient living city of a continuous civilization.

With a view to exploring the various facets of Kashi's cultural traditions I first of all surveyed the two most important institutions, namely, the institutions of ascetics and the pandits of traditional learning, which essentially provide a basic format to Kashi's sacred and secular traditions. While studying the sacred institution of ascetics I felt that this cannot be placed under an exclusive category of "sacred" as something opposite to "secular", or "profane". This raised volleys of questions on the nature of the sacred in Indian cultural traditions. These will have to be answered for a better comprehension of the sacred complex in Kashi.

FOUR NODAL POINTS

The smattering of Kashi, which I have acquired in the past few years, leads me to say that there are four nodal points from where the pageant of the sacred complex in Kashi can be viewed at a glance: (1) the cult of the *tirthas*, (2) the cult of Vishvanath, (3) the cult of the Ganga, and (4) the cult of the *shmashana*. The main areas of research and some of the basic questions which one may address oneself along these points can be briefly outlined as follows.

The cult of the tirthas

The sacred myth about Kashi has been described in the *Matsya Purana*, the *Vayu Purana*, the *Skanda Purana*, and various other *Puranas* and *Upa-Puranas*. The fourth chapter of the *Skanda Purana*, known as *Kashi Khanda*, gives the full description of Kashi-kshetra, indicating the names and locations of all the *tirthas*. It is said that all the *tirthas* of India are located in Kashi. It is also claimed by the knowledgeable sacred intellectuals that the present Kashi is the one described in the *Puranas* and that all the *tirthas* in Kashi are today located exactly in the manner described in the ancient scriptures. The archaeologists, on the other hand, claim that modern Kashi is of recent development and that ancient Kashi lies buried in the mounds scattered near Rajghat, at some distance. To what extent do these claims stand anthropological test? To what extent has the oral tradition been truly supported by textual tradition? How do the people hold this tradition? Is there a continuity in the *Pauranic* geography of Kashi? If so, how has this continuity been maintained?

According to the *Kashi Khanda*, the Kashi-kshetra is divided into three *khandas* (segments): (1) Vishveshvara-khanda, (2) Omkara-khanda, and (3) Kedara-khanda. How have the boundaries of these segments been marked or maintained? What are the myths associated with these *khandas*?

The various *tirthas* in Kashi are connected with one another by the sacred *Pauranic* myths. Can these *tirthas* be organizationally or attributionally linked as a single entity? What are the functions of the sacred myths in organizing pilgrimage to Kashi? Could these *tirthas* be arranged in an hierarchy of importance (as reflected in the sacred *Pauranic* myths and/or popularly exhibited in terms of pilgrims' visit to the shrines)?

A number of *tirthas* in Kashi have been abandoned/occupied by the householders for secular use. Who are these householders? How have they responded to their conscience? How have the religious minded people of Kashi reacted to it?

The social ecology of the *tirthas* has always provided

heterogeneous contents, so far as local, linguistic and caste groups are concerned. Whether these *tirthas* are managed on local patronage? To what extent are they relevant to the all-India pilgrims visiting Kashi? Could these be regarded as centres of local worship? Or could we arrange them in various orders of worship (*tirthas* of local importance, *tirthas* worshipped by devotees from various *mohallas* in Kashi, and *tirthas* worshipped by pilgrims from Uttar Pradesh villages and those by all-India pilgrims)?

The cult of Vishwanath

Vishwanath is the presiding God of Kashi. But there are four Vishwanath temples in the city: (1) *adi* Vishwanath, (2) golden temple of Vishwanath, (3) *naya* Vishwanath, and (4) Vishwanath temple in the precinct of the Banaras Hindu University. Of these, the first two are related to the *Jyotirlinga* (self-created effulgent *lingam*) complex. The first temple, *adi* Viswanath, claims to be the original place of *Jyotirlinga* whose temple was demolished by the Moslem rulers. The second temple claims to have enshrined the original *Jyotirlinga* which was re-installed by Maharani Ahilyabai of Indore in 1777 and whose temple was gilted by Maharana Ranjeet Singh in 1839. The third temple of Vishwanath was constructed with a view to preserving the pristine purity of God Vishwanath whose *linga* was supposedly polluted by the entry of Harijans in 1956. The fourth temple in the precinct of the Banaras Hindu University is famous for its colossal structure which is open to all, regardless of caste, sect and religion of the visitor.

That the place where the *Jyotirlinga* of Vishwanath was once enshrined continues to be a place of worship, although the present *linga* does not claim to be the *Jyotirlinga*. Why is this place still worshipped in the name of *adi* Vishwanath? What does this signify? The golden temple of Vishwanath has acquired popularity as the one enshrining the original piece of *Jyotirlinga*. It is hard to establish historically that the present *linga* is the one which has survived Moslem invasion. What is that which has led the people to uphold such belief? That the origin of *naya* Vishwanath temple indicates that the orthodox Brahmans have devaluated God in the golden temple of Vishwanath, but the latter continues to enjoy popularity. Why? Does it show that the concept of sacred has changed? That the fourth Vishwanath temple presents entirely a new situation; it is open to all Hindus and Moslems, and to Christians as well. Its popularity seems to be based largely on its architectural magnificence. But, is this all for which the pilgrims go there? From these the questions that arise are: Whether the Hindu concept of sacred is *sthanapradhan* (importance of place) or *vastupradhan* (importance of object)? What sustains the sacred myth of *Jyotirlinga*? Whether the four temples of Vishwanath present a case of hierarchy in the sacred? Whether and how the concept of sacred is changing in Hindu society?

The first two temples claim the merit of *Jyotirlinga* Vishwanath in a way which should naturally divide the people on the question of treating sacred as manifest in a place (*sthan*) or in an object (*vastu*). The third temple demolishes their claim by presenting an orthodox view of treating a sacred object. The fourth overruns the claims put forth by all the three and presents a new concept of the sacred which is all-embracing. Under the circumstances when each of these four temples presents four different concepts of the sacred, the pilgrims visiting Kashi are apparently led to a situation of cultural conflict, at least one of confusion—taking them in four directions. But will this lead them to a crisis or total loss of faith? Is this a case of Hindu society being led towards a fatal crash or an internal crisis of faith in transcendence, which has all along been a source of its vitality? Or, is this an illustration of the resilient Hindu society? To what extent do all the four Vishwanath temples differ among themselves on the processes of elaboration, idealization and perpetuation of Hindu sacred tradition both in depth and in spread?

The cult of the Ganga

The uniqueness of the river Ganga in Kashi, as common Hindus believe, lies in its physical form—its being *uttarvahini* and *ardhachandrakar*. That in other places its natural course is from north to south; in Kashi it flows from south to north. That its crescent form symbolises the moon brightening the *jata* (matted hair) of the lord Shiva. That it clings to the city of Vishwanath throughout the year. That the dirt and filth of the city are drained into the river and yet its water remains unpolluted, healthy and holy. That Kashi without Ganga is like a body without life, without soul.

Such feelings for the Ganga are clearly and comprehensively reflected in the ritual behaviour pattern of the pilgrims. Most of the important rituals are performed at the ghats on the river. What are these rituals and what aspects of life do they cover? Whether the rituals performed at the ghats are largely purificatory? To what extent are these rituals endowed with supreme religious merits such as *punya* (religious merits) and *moksha* (salvation)? Whether or not the river Ganga in Kashi forms a sacred complex independent of the cult of Vishwanath?

That the sacred intellectuals—ascetics and pandits—as also the priests and common Hindus live close to the Ganga. That the sacred territory of Kashi is formed along the course of the Ganga; and that the sacredness of a place in Kashi is dependent on its proximity to the river. That almost all important shrines of Kashi are located within this sacred territory. That the princely Hindu States from all over India have built ghats and magnificent buildings all along the river bank in this city. What is that which attracts people to settle close to the Ganga? To what extent has this concept of sacred territory integrated the people from diverse linguistic regions, sects and professions? What are the secular networks of integration that have developed mainly on account of sacred requirements? How far is the cultural landscape along the river an art of the sacred? To what extent does it exhibit the sense of aesthetic in the cultivation of the sacred?

That the people who earn their livelihood by performing rituals at the ghats call themselves Gangaputra (sons of the river Ganga). That the boatmen who ply boats in the river also regard themselves as the sons of the river Ganga. To what extent has this sacred mother been able to hold her two sons together as sacerdotalists? Whether the boatmen who are socially inferior to the Brahman priests have been able to raise their position in the sacred territory of the Ganga? Whether or not they have been given a role in the

12. The Varanasi ghats : Rana ghat, Darbhanga ghat

Facing Page 113

13. The Varanasi ghats : Manmandir ghat

Brahmanic ritual complex? If so, whether they are allowed to act as priests ritually at par with the Brahman Gangaputra?

Who are the people perpetuating the myths about the Ganga? What modes do they adopt? Whether the sacred myth about the Ganga finds its support from the cult of Vishwanath?

The cult of the shmashana

Kashi has been referred to in the *Puranas* as *Mahashmashana* (the great cremation place), the city of Shiva the *Mahakala* (the great destroyer). But the "great destroyer" in the city of Anandavana is *kalyankari* (auspicious). For, those who leave here their mortal bodies attain *moksha* at once. The belief is so deep-rooted that even when a person dies outside Kashi—in some cases thousand of miles away—his dead body is brought for cremation at the Manikarnika or Harischandra ghat.

There are several ways to attain *moksha*. While the other *tirthas* are the bestowers of *punya* which finally leads the pilgrims to the path of *moksha*, Kashi is the one which assures *moksha* to each and everyone dying within its precinct. How far has this belief added importance to Kashi as a *tirtha* excelling all other *tirthas* in India? When did this concept of "Kashi the *mokshadayini*" appear in the scriptures? It may be borne in mind that the Buddha preached for the first time the concept of *nirvana* at Sarnath, 8 km north of Kashi. The Brahmanic concept of *mokshadayini* Kashi might have developed as a challenge thrown to the Buddhist doctrine of *nirvana*, and hence it is likely to be a post-Buddha concept. But, at any rate, this has to be ascertained. One must also examine the concept of death as the most "auspicious one". How has it come in Indian scriptural traditions?

If the sacred death in Kashi is the bestower of *moksha* then how have the Hindu scriptures accounted for *papa* (sin) and *punya* as the deciding factors in man's liberation? How do people explain the theory of *karma* contextually? To what extent has this affected the social behaviour of an individual? How do people of Kashi conceptualise death? Whether the concept of the "sacred death" has brought about any change in the general pattern of Hindu mortuary rites?

There are two burning ghats in Kashi: one is the most celebrated Manikarnika which is believed to be permanent abode of Shiva and his consort Parvati, and another one is named after the *Pauranic* king *satyavadi* (truthful) Harischandra who is known to have served the king of Kashi who happened to be a Dom by caste. At these two ghats the Doms have a very important function, they offer the sacred fire for cremation, which even the highest of the Hindus accept. How is it that the Doms, who in Hindu society occupy the lowliest position (untouchables), have been given such an important and crucial role in man's highest achievement of *moksha*? How and when did these Doms become the custodian of the "sacred fire"? Is this belief held by all sections of Hindus? Is this a local custom? Has it got the scriptural sanction? How does Hindu society rationalise this paradox in its value system?

Cremation ghats are visited by Yogis and ascetics of various orders for acquiring "power", gaining transcendental knowledge. How does Hindu society treat the "sacred profane" opposition?

CONSUMERS OF THE SACRED

The foregoing description relates to the organization of the sacred; and, to some extent, it also provides a ground for understanding the nature of the sacred. But unless the consumers of the sacred—the citizens of Kashi and the pilgrims—are examined in the context of their participation in the sacred complex, the treatment of this subject shall remain incomplete and inconclusive. The levels of their participation have to be carefully examined, particularly on caste and regional basis. This can be done by recording (a) their daily routine, specifying their activities related to sacred performances and the distribution of time devoted to sacred/secular activities, and (b) their cultural bio-data.

To record the cultural bio-data of the citizens the following points may be covered: What places of pilgrimage has the informant visited? Does he/she follow any pilgrimage cycle? Note his/her existing knowledge of the sacred geography of Kashi—the beliefs related to the *tirthas* of Kashi. Also note the sources of such cultural knowledge. Whether he/she is a member of a religious institution, an academic institution, and/or a political party? Whether he/she has the requisite knowledge of the sacred performances? Whether or not the informant's sacred performances are confined to the sacred centres of his/her locality? Whether his/her association with the sacred centres is governed by linguistic, locational, or purely religious considerations? In addition to some of these relevant questions a few more specific questions can be put to the pilgrims from outside: How was he/she motivated to make a pilgrimage to Kashi? Whether he/she had read/heard the *mahatmya* (glory) of Kashi before undertaking this pilgrimage? In the present visit, what new things about the *mahatmya* of Kashi have been added to his/her knowledge? What are the sources of such knowledge, and how was it acquired? Note the informant's existing knowledge of the sacred geography of Kashi and the required sacred performances. Also note how much money the informant has actually spent on the performance of rituals, feeding Brahmans and beggars, and on buying ritual articles, sacred literature, and articles of secular use.

While some work has been done on pilgrims and pilgrimage practically nothing has been said so far on the participation of the common citizens in the sacred complex of a *tirtha*. Jha (1971) has given an interesting account of the *kutis* (abode of ascetics) and the participation of the ascetics in the sacred complex of Janakpur. The ascetics are a special group of people. There is a need to examine both the specialists and the generalists. There has also been a tendency to generalise the behaviour of the pilgrims. The implicit assumption is that all those who visit a place of pilgrimage interact fully and equally with the sacred phenomena operating there.

While this can be true about Mecca and Jerusalem, one can hardly find it in a Hindu place of pilgrimage like Kashi. What is important in the study of Hindu sacred complex is to find out how the *tirthas* integrate diverse cultural traditions into a common bond of civilization. This can be done most fruitfully by comparing the culturally patterned behaviour of both the citizens and the pilgrims.

HYPOTHESES

My personal experiences in Kashi lead me to frame the following hypotheses which may be tested in future studies of the sacred complex in India:

1. That Vidyarthi's concept of the "sacred complex" is widely applicable to the *Pauranic tirthas* of India.
2. That the elements of the "sacred complex" are formed on the basis of scriptural canons and upheld by a long and continuous tradition of sacred myth.
3. That in the process of its transmission, the scriptural sacred myth has acquired an omnibus character, accommodating varieties of textual and oral traditions.
4. That there is a continuity in the *Pauranic* sacred traditions in the *tirthas* of India.
5. That the organization and accretion of sacred complex are largely dependent on secular incentives and material progress.
6. That the sacred is the energising force in Hindu mode of cultivating excellence.
7. That in Indian cultural tradition there is a sacred-secular continuum which can be observed in all the three elements of sacred complex, noted by Vidyarthi.
8. That the diacritical marks in the sacred complex are culturally patterned; and hence in essence the sacred complex symbolises the totality of cultural traditions.
9. That the sacred complex is raised on various layers of cultural complexes and hence different ethnic groups in Hindu society do not interact with the Brahmanic sacred complex fully and equally at a point of time.
10. That the *tirthas* of India are culturally distinguishable from one another as local, regional and all-India centres of sacred complexes.
11. That such spatial distinctions may be located even in a single *tirtha* of all-India importance.
12. That these spatial categories are formed both in textual and in oral cultural traditions.
13. That in the treatment of the sacred complex in a place of pilgrimage the producer and the consumer of the

sacred as also the citizens and pilgrims stand apart, and that it is this gap which truly indicates their "reality culture".

OUTLINE OF CULTURAL MATERIALS

The following outline is suggested for analysing the cultural materials on the sacred complex:

1. Sacred geography

1.1. *Pauranic*/geographic data.

1.1.1. *Pauranic* references in the chronological order.

1.1.2. Persistence and change in *Pauranic* geography.

1.1.3. Concept of sacred territory and boundary maintenance mechanism.

1.2. Sacred architecture and the installation of deities—order and preference.

1.3. Cultural ecology—temples, sacred wells and tanks, etc.

1.3.1. Use of social space, distribution of classified population (caste, language, sect or religion) and occupation.

1.3.2. Historical events shaping cultural landscape.

2. Sacred specialists

2.1. Sacred intellectuals/theorists—their organization and training.

2.2. Practising ritual specialists—nature of specialization, their organization and training, their relationship with theorists.

2.3. Ritual associates—nature and extent of association, their organization and training, their relationship with the ritual specialists.

2.4. Sacred specialists in the secular context—organization of occupation (ownership, distribution of income), patronage, clientele; occupational change and style of life.

2.5. Specialists *vis-a-vis* generalists—the system of classification (textual, contextual); attitude towards the sacred; the specialists' awareness of being a special class of people and their sense of responsibility towards their sacerdotal function; the role and rank of specialists in Hindu society and the levels of their interaction (caste, language, sect) with the generalists; their mode of integrating the generalists.

3. **Sacred performances**

3.1. Organization of sacred performance.

3.1.1. Home performance in a shrine—daily, special; regional variation according to the owner of the shrine; nature and mode of elaboration and its impact on the devotees.

3.1.2. Types of specialists required in a single performance—*yajna*, *abhiseka*, *samskara*, etc.

3.2. Textually prescribed rituals and the mode of performances—normal, exceptional cases.

3.3. Orally transmitted ritual—performer and helper.

3.4. Objects of performances—classification based on social requirements and personal situation; the motive of the performer (*dharma*, *artha*, *kama*, *moksha*); variation in age, sex, sanskritic knowledge and economic condition of the performer.

3.5. Attributes of the sacred and the requirements of performances—offerings (preference, taboo), unique features.

3.6. Symbolism of offerings—ritual articles and mode of performances.

3.7. Aesthetics of the sacred performance—selection of items, method or performance.

3.8. Individual and congregational performances—variation in modes and contents; caste, sect and linguistic consideration.

3.9. Content analysis of the sacred performances—number of rites in a single performance; local, regional and all-India performances; their Vedic, *Pauranic* and local origin and distribution.

3.10. Ideal pilgrimage—textual prescription, regional variation, socio-cultural levels of participation.

3.11. Continuity and change in sacred performances—rules regarding eligibility (personal purity, caste, sect consideration); use of Sanskrit text, duration and frequency of performance, assistance of specialists required; use of ritual articles and offerings.

4. Sacred myth

4.1. *Pauranic*/textual myth regarding the origin and the *mahatmya* of the *tirtha.*

4.2. Oral tradition regarding the origin and the *Mahatmya* of the *tirtha*—variation according to caste, linguistic group, ritual specialists and generalists.

4.3. Transmission of the sacred myth regarding the *mahatmya* of the place, object of worship, ritual articles, and ritual offerings (modes and media).

4.4. Use of sacred myth in secular context—curing of disease, social gathering and politicization.

4.5. Impact of sacred myths on personal and social behaviour—*dana,* cultivating fellow-feeling.

4.6. Content analysis of the sacred myths.

5. Nature of the sacred

5.1. Sacred as the great healer.

5.2. Sacred as the energising force in man's creativity.

5.3. Sacred as an industry.

5.4. Sacred as an integrating element.

5.5. Sacred as the vehicle of traditions.

5.6. Sacred-secular continuum.

Although the foregoing outline of cultural materials has been prepared on the basis of the data on the sacred complex in Kashi, it may be applied equally to any other place of Hindu pilgrimage.

REFERENCES

Jha, Makhan 1971. *Sacred Complex in Janakpur.* Allahabad.

Vidyarthi, L.P. 1961. *The Sacred Complex in Hindu Gaya.* Bombay.

7

FUNCTIONS OF A SACRED CITY

MOST historians have pointed out that urbanization in India is a post-Moslem phenomenon. Few have attempted to report on the cultural processes of the structural growth of Indian towns and cities. It is not surprising, therefore, that the historians of culture have failed to comprehend fully the difference between the pre- and the post-Moslem operation of the urban systems in India. To say how weak and generalized their concept is, it may be stated that the post-Moslem towns in India are comparatively small in number; they have grown from the seats of administration, trade, commerce and industries. Traditional Indian towns, on the contrary, have evolved from places of pilgrimage—the centres of learning, the beauteous surroundings—hills, forests, river-fords, and sea-coasts. Unlike the 'modern' commercial cities which asphyxiate themselves with fumes, the places of pilgrimage are fascinated by "decoration of light, the aethereal aromas of flowers, incense and sandalwood paste, the melody of prayer and the splendour of temple music—all that make one experience the overwhelming pleasure, the supreme bliss". (Saraswati 1976). At these places both "sacred" and "secular" institutions have developed simultaneously. These have also been the centres of our civilizations. They are marked off from villages by their settlement pattern, economic activities, style of life, social institutions, and interpersonal relationships. They may not be the prototypes of the *nagaras* described by Kautilya and

Vatsyayana, but are undoubtedly good examples of the *Pauranic tirtha nagaras* (sacred cities). However, the purpose of this essay is not to draw comparison between the traditional and the modern models of the urban form, but to highlight the functions of a sacred city, which may also broadly indicate how different they are in their structural designs and cultural focus.

In dealing with this subject I rely heavily upon my own data on Kashi (Saraswati 1975)—my life project. Since there is nothing yet on record to show that the situation in other sacred cities is different, I begin with this assumption that the four-fold functions which Kashi admirably demonstrates are most fundamental in respect of all the sacred cities of India.

CULTURAL PATTERNING

One of the important functions of a sacred city is the patterning of cultures. Like all cities, the population of a sacred city is heterogeneous. But, unlike others, it does not attempt at the uniformization of people. Instead, it builds up a democracy of cultures. In Kashi, for instance, people from all over India are settled in linguistic clusters such as of Tamilians, Karnatakas, Bengalis, Maithils, Nepalis, Maharashtrians, Gujaratis, Panjabis, Sindhis, and local Uttar Pradeshis, each preserving its identity in respect of food, dress, language, rituals, ceremonies, and shrines. In respect of rituals there are varieties of traditions such as Vedic, *Tantric*, and *Laukic*, observable in local and regional customs of worship as also in the objects of offerings. For instance, the South Indians perform *kum-kum archana* in the Annapoorna temple, but others do not observe this ritual. One of the rites peculiar to the Nepalis is that pigeons are brought to the temple precinct and set free in the name of the worshipper. To the small-pox deity Sheetala, the South Indians offer coconut and boiled rice, the Bengalis sacrifice only boiled rice, while the local Uttar Pradeshis offer *halwa* and *puri*. Most of the regional groups maintain personal shrines where worship and performances are made according to their respective traditions. Thus, there are South Indian temples, Bengali temples, Maithil temples, Gujarati, Maharashtrian, Nepali, and Rajasthani temples, distinguishable in architectural form, patronage and modes of worship. There are varieties of ritual specialists in Kaṣhi, each having a distinct function in the organization of pilgrimage and ritual performances. These specialists belong to different linguistic groups, castes, and classes. They maintain their caste and linguistic character in pristine purity but interact closely with the pilgrims from all over India.

The citizens of Kashi as also the pilgrims visiting Kashi belong to three types of cultural traditions: oral (*laukic*), textual (*shastric*), and transcendental (*naivritic*) (Saraswati 1970, 1972). To an Ahir or a Dom, belonging to the Oral Cultural Tradition, what is important is to make a special worship of the non-Brahmanic shrines of deified heroes called *birs* such as Agiyabir, Lahurabir, and Dautrabir with whom the city abounds. His participation in the worship at the Brahmanic shrines or *devasthals*, which are central to the people of the Textual Cultural Tradition, is minimal and of secondary importance. Then there are ascetics of the Transcendental Cultural Tradition to whom the worship of an idol or a visit to a shrine is neither required nor significant. To them, ideally, there is no distinction between what others call 'sacred' and 'profane'. Thus, there are varieties of sacred traditions which Kashi encompasses within its fold.

In brief, Kashi appears as mini-India, accommodating varieties of peoples and cultures, allowing each of them to maintain its distinctiveness and to grow according to its respective traditions. This sort of cultural patterning has been possible because of the belief reflected in the social organization of this sacred city that there are various ways to unite with the ultimate and one can choose the way one likes.

INTEGRATION OF CULTURES

The belief which lies at the root of cultural differences is also the potent factor integrating the heterogeneous cultures.

The myth that all the thirtythree hundred million gods and goddesses reside in Kashi denotes the all-embracing character of this sacred city. Kashi presents the totality of Hindu sacred tradition. It accommodates all its variant strands. The fact that all the *sampradayas* have their tutelary deities in Kashi and that all of them hold this city equally in high esteem bears out the testimony of cultural tolerance.

Another belief which integrates the varieties of Indian cultural traditions is "Kashi the *mokshadayani*". It is believed that Kashi is the place where one gets *moksha* by just leaving one's mortal body at the cremation ghat of Manikarnika. This belief which guarantees salvation has induced the Hindu believers from all parts of India to come to this place, alive or dead. It is on the basis of this single belief that Kashi has become a truly cosmopolitan city; has developed a composite culture; and has built up a grand tradition. This belief has a far-reaching consequence. By implication it means that the citizens of Kashi just cannot afford to be parochial (a very unfortunate phenomenon which now stifles our modern urban society). They cannot stop people from other regions of India to settle down in Kashi unless they prefer Kashi to lose the universality of its sacred belief which is the axis of its continual functioning, its very life force.

The institution of pilgrimage has also a levelling influence on the diverse social life. Sex, colour, civil condition, economic inequality, traditions of servitude which have made some people untouchables become unreal distinctions in course of pilgrimage. For instance, it is here that a Brahman—the tallest in the society—comes to the Manikarnika ghat and asks for the sacred fire from its custodian—the untouchable Dom—because without this sacred fire his deceased kinsman cannot attain *moksha*—the supreme sacred. A man in the highest office or in possession of fabulous wealth stoops to touch the feet of a semi-literate pauper priest (*tirtha purohita*)—a ritual without which he cannot acquire the desired *tirthaphala*. It is only during the pilgrimage that the unity of faith and social solidarity in Hindu society and religion can be seen at its best.

In brief, it is through the network of pilgrimage that Kashi operates as a civilizational centre. And it is by this mechanism that Indian civilization has been integrating all through the ages its geographical and cultural diversities.

CULTIVATION OF EXCELLENCE

The third important function of the sacred city is to cultivate excellence in varieties of creative arts and literature. Most of Kashi's secular arts and crafts such as ivory and brasswork, *kalabattu* and weaving, perfume making, and culinary art for which Kashi has been famous through the ages, have flourished on account of pilgrim industry. The pilgrims' continual inflow in Kashi provides a good market for the varieties of utilitarian and luxury goods. Pilgrims visiting Kashi spend the major portion of their budget on buying *Banarasi sarees*, toys, cosmetics, brass utensils, and ritual articles.

Kashi has produced several world-fame musicians, both Hindus and Moslems. These luminaries had made the shrines and ghats, and *mathas* and *akharas* of Kashi their centres of *sadhana*. In the schools of Indian music the Banaras *gharana* of Kashi stands in high favour.

It was the sacred myth of Kashi that attracted pandits from all over India to settle here. This eventually led to the cultivation of excellence in various fields of traditional learning. It was the attraction of Kashi that brought Santa Tulsidas to compose here at the banks of the Ganga his celebrated *Ramayana*. Many other saints and scholars with whom this sacred city of the Hindus still abounds come here to spend last days of their lives. All of them have contributed in their own way to the grand tradition of Kashi.

Let no one be mistaken that Kashi is only the city of *moksha*—the other worldly culture. In fact, in its self-identifiable culture *moksha* is not the dominant theme. As a cultural group, the people of Kashi address themselves by the term *Banarasi*. A person belonging to the *Banarasi* culture has a distinct style of life identifiable by his dress, food, drink, speech, manners, sense of humour and habits. A *Banarasi* is aware of his unique style of life and when he goes out of his city he finds in the new surroundings certain forms of expressions of his life missing. What is missing there is the *Banarasiness* which his city alone can provide. His self-conscious 'oneness' that he commonly displays in his interaction with others arises out of this consideration and hence *Banarasi* is his 'reality culture'. Thus, it comes out that what is dominant in the 'reality culture' of Kashi is the *bhoga* which characterizes excellence in material culture as reflected in the way of life of a *banarasi*—an exemplary life worth living.

In brief, a sacred city is not only a place of *moksha* but also of *bhoga*, that is to say, it gives equal emphasis to the spiritual and to the material development of man and society.

PRESERVATION OF IDEAL TYPES

The fourth and the most important function of a sacred city of the Hindus is the preservation of 'ideal types' which serve as an index to the grandeur of a civilization. In Kashi, nearly two thousand ascetics of all varieties reside permanently; besides there is a floating stream of ascetic pilgrims. This means, the proportion of ascetics to the total Hindu population of the city is nearly 1 : 150, or one out of every two hundred forty of the total population of Kashi is an ascetic. In Hindu society ascetics have been compared with *dhruvatara* (pole star), because they symbolize the highest ideal which the *grihis* (householders) must try to attain.

Besides the ascetics, there are large numbers of pandits who are not only great scholars but also the champions of orthodox traditions. They lead austere life and exemplify the ideal type of Brahmans and sages described in ancient scriptures.

The overall impact of religion on the life and ways of the citizens of Kashi is too great, regardless of their heterogeneous social categories, diverse educational background, and varied professional specialization. The intensity of their faith in the sacred tradition of Kashi can be judged by the fact that hundred per cent of Hindu citizens (including babies in their mother's arms) visit temples and take bath at the holy ghats. Most of them perform regularly varieties of rites such as *Ganga-pujan*, *abhiseka* to Vishwanath, Vishwanath-*darshan*, weekly *darshan* of some important deities, *sringararati-darshan*, *antargrihi parikrama*, *panchakroshi-parikrama*, *charodham-parikrama*, *Brahman-bhojan*, *madhukari* to *sannyasis*, *kangali-bhojan*, *pindadan*, *havana*, and arranging *katha-kirtan* at sacred centres and/or at home. Although comparable data are not available yet it cannot be said with the same confidence that the Hindu citizens of any other 'secular' town reflect such a high degree of religiosity as one finds among the people of Kashi.

Thus, from the point of view of leading a religion-oriented

life the citizens of Kashi definitely represent the ideal type. As mentioned earlier, they also strike a balance between *moksha* and *bhoga*. This creates in them (the *Banarasis*) a condition of ethical existential reality.

CONCLUSION

In conclusion we might say that a sacred city functions in varieties of ways towards building a culture of democracy, a federation of human faiths, a centre of excellence, and a paradisal place for the preservation of the highest human ideals. All 'secular' cities accommodate heterogeneous population and produce excellence in varieties of fields. But whether they integrate their citizens, both emotionally and culturally, to the extent a sacred city does or whether they offer that excellent quality of life—*masti*, *akkhadpan* and *phakkadpan*—which characterize a *Banarasi* of Kashi is a question that awaits exploration. The study of Kashi has, however, left us in no doubt that the sacred cities of India serve a cathartic and almost a therapeutic function of allaying the strains and stresses of urban life; and hence their relevance today.

REFERENCES

Saraswati, Baidyanath 1970. *Contributions to the Understanding of Indian Civilization*. Dharwar.

Saraswati, Baidyanath 1972. Sacred complexes in Indian cultural traditions. In B.C. Agarwal (ed.) *Anthropological Approaches to the Study of a Complex Society*. Delhi.

Saraswati, Baidyanath 1975. *Kashi : Myth and Reality of a Classical Cultural Tradition*. Simla.

Saraswati, Baidyanath 1976. Anthropological approach to the study of religions. In Surajit Chandra Sinha (ed.) *Anthropology in India : Cultural Anthropology*. Calcutta.

8

THE HOLY CIRCUIT OF NAIMISARANYA

SITUATED on the left bank of the river Gomati at the junction of Khairabad and Sitapur road on the latitude 27°26′ north and longitude 80°35′ east, the little town of Naimisaranya or Nimsar is a picturesque place of Hindu pilgrimage. It is 38 km from Sitapur (Uttar Pradesh) by rail. The town is famous for its Chakra-kunda (sacred well) and the fables connected with it. On every new-moon day a large number of people flock to purify their bodies in the holy waters of the well. If the new-moon falls on Monday, it is believed that a holy bath in Chakra-kunda and offering to the presiding deity Lalita will wash away all the sins committed in life-time. About 10,000 celebrants gather on this occasion. The most interesting and important congregation is seen on the *Shivratri*-day in *Phalgun* when the people meet for *parikrama* or the round of pilgrimage which lasts for 15 days. Perhaps, nowhere in India such an interminable *parikrama* of 269 km is undertaken. Though people from different parts of India come to join this, the peasants of Uttar Pradesh outnumber others.

MYTHOLOGICAL ORIGIN

Naimisaranya is a living repository of peasant faith. In spite of its origin being lost in antiquity, the peasants are able to trace its hoary past through legends and scriptures. The legend which bears the origin of the sanctity of this place goesli ke this:

Once a delegation of 88 thousand sages headed by the great sage Shaunaki, sedulous of knowing the most sacred place on the earth, called on the God Brahma who reposed upon the snowy mountain top. All the sages and the Devas sang the saga of the Creator and prayed that He may please vouchsafe to bring forward to them the place on the earth to be most commendable to religious worship. Pleased by their *stuti* (devotional prayer and songs) the drowsy Brahma took a *chakra* (discus) and whirling it in the air directed it to proceed in search. After going round all the four *lokas* and the whole earth the discus finally rested at a place near the river Gomati, which thenceforth took the name of Naimisaranya. Following the discus there came the sages, the Devtas and Brahma himself. The discus penetrating the earth entered *patal* (the nether-world) and a fountain burst out which grew into the famous Chakra-kunda. The Brahma indicated that it was to be the most sacred place and the centre of the earth.[1] He then summoned to the place some 33 crores of *tirthas* or the ministering angels, each of whom presides over his special place of religious worship. All these *tirthas* settled down at places within 16 km of the central point (Naimisaranya). Since then this place has got an immortal sanctity; and the tradition has it that Rama after his expedition against the demon king, Ravana of Lanka, came here to bathe in the Chakra-kund in order to wash away the sin of having killed a Brahman in the person of Ravana.

THE SACRED SHRINES

Enriched by beautiful scenery of the river Gomati and tropical vegetation, the little Naimisaranya is hallowed by her association with the life of *Maharshi* Vyas, the author of the Vedas and the son of the great *Rishi* Parasar and his spouse Satyawati. It is said that the *Maharshi* transcribed his work in Naimisaranya and his *gaddi* (the sacred seat) is still worshipped here in his memory. Naimisaranya encloses within her precincts the holiest cemetery of Swayambhuaw Manu and his wife Shatrupa. In suchwise, there are several temples, sacred mounds or other

14. The Varanasi ghats : Scindia ghat

15. The Varanasi ghats : Panchaganga ghat

natural shrines and bathing ghats which constitute the sacred geography of Naimisaranya.

Though every atom of Naimisarnya is sacred and solemn, the most celebrated places are the Chakra-kund or Chakra tirtha and the temple of Lalita Devi. The *Chakra-kund* is a circular sacred well burrowed by the *chakra* of Brahma, where the devout take a purificatory bath to be freed from all sins. Happy is a Hindu who dies in the sacred ground of Naimisaranya after taking a holy bath in Chakra-kunda, for he is transported at once to Lord Vishnu's blissful paradise. Offering of *pindas* to the ancestors, ritual hair cropping of the child, and donating to Brahmans in this *tirtha* are credited as most gainfully sacrosanct.

Lalita Devi, the presiding female deity of this *tirtha*, has widespread celebrity. She is the granter of desire. She grants health, wealth and progeny. The barren woman stoops to seek the pleasure of Lalita Devi who will grant her a child. Physical ailments like eye-diseases, cholera and small-pox are healed by this deity. Men who are suffering from eye-disease will offer a silver or golden eye to the deity—an eye given and an eye got. White flowers, sweets, cloves, *chhatra* (crown), silver eyes and colourful clothes are the sacred offerings the deity Lalita is propitiated with. "Such is the stamina of belief", says an informant, "that the votary whose life is saved by the grace of this deity will offer the tip of his tongue as a token of profound reverence, and the miracle is that his tongue becomes all right over-night."

THE PRIEST

The officiating priests of these shrines are called the Pandas who are the Ganga-Putra Brahmans. The institution and function of these Pandas are similar to those found elsewhere in India. They hold a traditional monopoly over the performance made here. Barring the temple of Lalita Devi, the Pandas have an almost exclusive right over the income of the shrines.

The temple of Lalita Devi has been the subject of a long controversy. Chota Mali told the writer that the present idol of the goddess Lalita belonged to his forefathers, and that

Lalita is one of the seven Devis (Phoolmati, Agarmati, Paharmati, Shitala Devi, Kshemkaya, Saraswati, and Lalita) of whom the Mali (gardener) community is the official priest. But the towering popularity of Lalita Devi called the attention of the greedy Pandas who later became hostile towards the Malis. There was a prolonged litigation. Several criminal cases were instituted against both the parties. The Pandas while claiming their rights denied the authority of the Malis in the temple of Lalita Devi. After a long trial the district court of Sitapur, pronounced the judgment that the income of Lalita's temple shall be equally distributed among the Malis and the Pandas. Recently, a committee has been appointed for the maintenance of the temple. On big religious occasions like *Somawati* and *Phalguni Amavasy a*when the number of ritual visitors is considerably very large, the income of the temple is leased out by contract.

One profitable practice, which some Brahmans have adopted, is to carry a mimic idol of Lalita Devi in a cloth-bound temple of miniature size from village to village and door to door. Such Brahmans are called Dolha Pandas, and they are looked down upon by the Brahmans and other Pandas of the main temple. All such Dolha Pandas are concentrated in three villages, namely Puraina, Ramkot and Beniganj—all around Naimisaranya.

THE ROUND OF PILGRIMAGE

The great Naimisaranya-kshetra is augmented in the radius of 16 km where all the sacred shrines of India are believed to be imbedded. The circumambulation of the *kshetra* performed by the great *Rishi* Dadhichi added its notability to a greater degree. As it says:

> Once there was an incessant battle between the Devas and the demons, and all the time the Devas were defeated by the deceitful demons. Alarmed by their defeat the Devas went to implore the aid of God Brahma. Brahma said that the only way to vanquish the demons was to use the bones of the sage Dadhichi as arms. Indra, the king of the Devas, took the task of approaching the *Rishi* for his

bones. He called upon the *Rishi* who was then in his hermitage at Misrikh, 9 km north of Naimisaranya. The great sage, apprised of Indra's intentions, said that he would be indeed very proud of sacrificing his body in so holy a cause, but unfortunately he had vowed to bathe at all the sacred shrines of India before he died and he must keep up his vow. God Indra returned to his celestial kingdom utterly disappointed, giving up all hopes of his victory. Brihaspati, the preceptor of gods, informed of Indra's anxiety, went to him and said that the angels of all the holy shrines of India had been established at and around Naimisaranya by Brahma himself, and if the Devas carried water from all the sacred places over which they presided and poured it over the old sage, the latter's vow would be fulfilled. Beaming with joy God Indra galloped to the *Rishi* and told him the solution on which the large-hearted sage expressed his satisfaction. Before surrendering his body for the sacrifice he walked round the Naimisaranya-kshetra, performing a holy *parikrama* of 169 km and then allowed a cow to lick his body to death. The Devas armed themselves with his bones and attacked the demons forthwith and gained an easy victory.

To commemorate this unmitigated sacrifice of the noble sage every year a large number of pilgrims perform the *parikrama* of Naimisaranya-kshetra in the month of *Phalgun.* The pilgrims commence their journey at little Naimisaranya on the new-moon day and traversing clock-wise on a circular route of 269 km for 11 days finally reach Misrikh where after 4 days' halt, the pilgrimage is brought to conclusion. The *parikrama* route defines the sacred ground of Naimisaranya-kshetra, the great Naimisaranya, and is protracted in the radius of 16 km from the central point Naimisaranya. The river Gomati cleaves out the *parikrama* circle. The Pandas of Naimisaranya and Misrikh divide their *jajamani* zones on the course of the river. The Pandas of Naimisaranya move with their respective patrons from Naimisaranya and leave them at Pipari. Crossing the river, the pilgrims are received in Deoganwana by the vigilant Pandas of Misrikh, who escort them along the rest of their journey. The Naimisaranya Pandas have no right to cross the river (at Pipari) with their patrons on ritual business, the breach of which will lead to an open quarrel.

Going round Naimisaranya on pilgrimage is a most blissful and felicitous experience. The pilgrims move in a procession accompanied by drummers, musicians and *kirtan mandalis*. The prestigious wealthy mendicants mounted on elephants lead the procession. The merchants on their camels, the Thakurs on their horses and the common peasants in their *laharus* (bullock-carts) come out to join the party. The old and fragile men sit in a *pinas* (palanquin). But, some orthodox pilgrims prefer to go on foot, for pilgrimage on foot is treated with special merit. In the thick of the processionists are the Pandas, the escorts and the ritual guides, who help the pilgrims in performing the worship of the sacred shrines which fall on the holy circuit. There are altogether 24 shrine villages (excluding the little towns of Naimisaranya and Misrikh) where several temples, mounds, sacred trees, and wells are worshipped.

The pilgrims are received by the people of the shrine villages, which fall *en route* along the *parikrama*, with great affection and reverence. Each village eagerly awaits its turn to receive the *parikrama* pilgrims and many of the villagers go to the extent of begging the dust of the feet of the sacred pilgrims. The villagers extend all kinds of possible helps to the pilgrims. In the paraw village, where the pilgrims have night halt, the pilgrims are provided with fire-wood, milk, sweets, vegetables, rice and other eatables. Some rich men give *bhandaras* (sumptuous charity feasting) to the pilgrims. The pilgrims who do not accept the charity may have their own arrangements. A mobile fair moves with the pilgrims and necessary things may be bought from it.

The journey, though long and tiresome, is most inspiring and rejoicing. All along the way, the musicians play on their traditional musical instruments (like *turhi*, *narsinha*, *sankh*, *mridang*, *dholak*, *ghariyal*, *dhap*, *jhanjh* and *damaru*, etc.), entertaining the weary travellers. The day passes in travelling and worship and the night comes for rest. But the enthusiastic pilgrims will not rest, and story telling and singing of devotional songs go on till late in the night. Thus roving about for 11 days the pilgrims finally reach Misrikh to conclude their pilgrimage. After 4 days' stay in Misrikh the pilgrims return home with joy and satisfaction of blotting out their sins, further transmitting the ritual of *parikrama* from generation to generation.

The *parikrama* rules are a few; these are both liberal and democratic. The *parikrama* is open to all. There is no caste restriction on going to the pilgrimage. Women are allowed. Only expectant and nursing mothers are not encouraged to join the *parikrama*. Even a menstruating women can join; but sexual-intercourse during these days is treated with great stringency. There is the interdiction that a woman thus conceiving shall give birth to a blind and deformed child; and after her death she will be granted hell to live in along with her sexual partner. As regards restrictions of food, non-vegetarian meals are strictly prohibited. Some virtuous pilgrims prefer to live only on fruits and milk during the *parikrama* days, and avoid salt. Giving charity to the Brahmans and other virtuous deeds on this occasion are fraught with positive virtues. It is believed, if the holy *parikrama* of Naimisaranya is once done in life the performer will not have to come into this world anymore, and will ever remain in the company of gods. If one is unable to join the *chaurasi kroshi parikrama* (the *parikrama* of the great Naimisaranya), he must do at least the *sawa kroshi parikrama* of the little Naimisaranya (going round the little Naimisaranya and covering the distance of 4 km). In the case of senility and extreme helplessness, one can depute someone on his or her behalf to perform the *parikrama*. The *punya* (or the merit) obtained by the *parikrama* is transferable. In return of the *punya* the appointer shall have to meet the expenses of the nominee which he or she will require for the pilgrimage. Such transference of *punya* is found, also in the case of ritual fasting, as is prevalent among the Maithil Brahmans. No elaborate ceremony is observed for the transference of *punya*.

OBSERVATIONS

Wherever the custom of circumambulation exists[2] it is observed with a religious or magical significance. For a Hindu circumambulation around certain sacred spots has the effect of blotting out sins. In the foregoing pages we have seen that the great *Rishi* Dadhichi walked round the Naimisaranya-kshetra before he sacrificed his mortal body for a holy cause, and since that day every year Naimisaranya has been circumambulated by thousands of Hindu pilgrims with a belief that it will wash away the sins committed in their life-time.[3] Besides this sacred aspect, the holy circumambulation of Naimisaranya lays open a very significant track in social phenomena, weaving the web of relationships among the 'sacred' and the 'secular' folk confederated in ritual interaction.

Naimisaranya serves as a nucleus for transmission of the great tradition to the Hindu peasants. By going round the pilgrimage for a fortnight the pilgrims are drawn to a structural relationship with the priestly organisation of Naimisaranya and Misrikh and of the shrine villages which fall on the holy circuit. This helps them in cultivating and inculcating the Hindu great tradition. It also provides an opportunity to the people of different ethnic and economic groups to unite for a sacred cause where all, regardless of caste and sex, stand in parity. Pilgrimage is a sacred act and hence those who go for pilgrimage are all sacred.

NOTES

1. The people and Pandas of Bithoor (a place of pilgrimage situated 22 km north of Kanpur) decline to accept that Naimisaranya is the centre of the earth. They hold that Bithoor is the centre of the earth and Brahma as a matter of course had thrust a nail there, which is preserved even to this day.
2. The custom of circumambulation is widely spread over. References of this custom are found in early Vedic literature. Circumambulation is figured on various occasions like initiation, marriage and funeral ceremonies. It is well-known among the Buddhists, particularly those of Tibet and Japan. The Greeks, the Romans, the Celts and the Gauls were all familiar with this custom. The evidence of circumambulation is found also in ancient Egypt. The

Muslims even to this day walk several times round the Kaba at Mecca and Oriental Christians perform the same ceremony round the Holy Sepulchre at Jerusalem.

3. Like Naimisaranya there are many other sacred places, viz., Janakpur (birth-place of Sita, a village on the Indo-Nepal border), Bithoor (Kanpur), Mathura, Kashi etc., where the devout Hindus go for circumambulation. Sometimes a sacred hill or river is also walked round by the pilgrims with the same object. The Hindus as well as the Jains go round the Girnar hill which is situated close to Junagadh town. The little hillock Barda in Jamnagar district is also circumambulated by the Hindu pilgrims. Circumambulation of the Narmada river is believed to be endowed with many virtues.

9

TEMPLE ORGANIZATION IN GOA

THE PORTUGUESE landed on the western coast of India in the beginning of the 16th century A.D. They captured the island of Goa from Adil Shah in the year 1510, remained in power till 1961, when Goa was absorbed in the Republic of India. This prolonged impact of the Portuguese for over 450 years has had an obvious effect on the social life of the Goanese; but some of the Hindus succeeded in retaining their religion intact. The force which guided the Hindus in the days of adversity, was, perhaps, their association with the temples and the deities enshrined therein. In the following pages an attempt has been made to describe briefly the organization of one of these temples, namely the temple of Shri Shanta Durga.

TEMPLES

There are several Hindu temples in the territory of Goa; but the most important and magnificent temples are situated in the districts of Ponda and Bicholim. The two noteworthy temples in Bicholim are the temples at Shirgao and Narora. The Shirgao temple is famous for its annual fair in which the Dhonds (peasant devotees) walk across and over a heap of burning coal of a bonfire without any burning injury to their feet. The temple of Saptakoteshvar at Narora was built by Shivaji, the founder of the Maratha Empire. This temple is commonly known as the *tirtha*. The district of Ponda contains the largest and best Hindu temples in Goa. Shri Ramnath, Shri Mahalakshmi and Shri Nagesh temples at Bandora, Shri Kamaksha temple at Siroda, Shri Mahalsa at Mardol, Shri Devakikrishna at Marcela and Shri Ganapati at Chandola are well-known in the district. But excelling them all in merit and magnificence are the temples of Shri Shanta Durga at Queula and the temple of Shri Mangesh situated at Priol; the two most important deities of the Gaud-Saraswat Brahmans of Goa.

Though none of the above temples has intricate carvings found in temples elsewhere in India, they are for the most part inviting and conspicuous because of the panoramic natural beauty they are surrounded with. Most of the temples are built in cool, shady and secluded places. Every temple has its own fairs and festivals which attract devotees from distant places. All these temples in general have the following eight typical characters:

(1) *Khamba* (post for lamps)
(2) *Tolli* (sacred tank of sweet water with steps all round)
(3) *Sthala* (a common ground-plan)
(4) *Chouko* (central rectangle meant for the priest)
(5) *Garbhakud* (the sanctuary where pilgrims perform *pradakshina* or circumambulation
(6) *Ghuda* (dome)
(7) *Gana* (secondary deity posted at the entrance of the temple to guard it from evil spirits)
(8) *Agrashala* (residential quarters for pilgrims).

Nothing definite, however, can be said about the age of these temples.

GAUD-SARASWATS AND THEIR DEITIES

As the legend goes, Parashuram, the great Brahman sage, conquered the territory of Shurparak by the sea-route. Shurparak is said to have been of the form of a winnowing fan, 400 *kroshas* (1280 km) in length and 12 *kroshas* (38 km) in breadth. Today, this place is known as Konkan. It is said that the sage brought 60 families of Brahmans from Trihottrapur, a place in the Bengal-Mithila region (Trihottrapur is a generic name for Tirhut, an administrative division of Bihar and part of Mithila). These Brahmans were called Gaud-Saraswat, because they came from Gaud and first settled on the banks of the Sarasvati river. All these Brahmans belonged to ten different *gotras* (clan), namely Bharadwaj, Kaushik, Vatsa, Kaundilya, Kashyap, Vashishta, Jamdagni, Vishvamitra, Gautama and Atri. They had their own *Kuladeva* (lineage deity) which they brought with them, and in whose honour they built temples in their settlements. The Brahmans of Kaushik *gotra*, who were brought to Goa, received the grant of the village extending from Kardalipur to Kelshi, now Quelossim in the administrative area of Mormugao. The deity, Shri Shanta Durga, installed in that village, belongs to these Brahmans. Similarly, Shri Mangesh is the lineage deity of the Brahmans belonging to Vatsa and Kaundilya *gotras* and the village Kushasthali or Kudthal (now Cortalim in the administrative area of Mormugao) was granted to them. Since that time the members belonging to the lineages of the founder Brahmans continue to adore their *Kuladeva*; and now, they are often referred to by the term *Mahajan* of their deity.

Like all other deities in the Hindu pantheon, the deities of Gaud-Saraswats too have their origin in some fascinating legends. Shri Shanta Durga is believed to have appeared in the course of a violent battle between Shiva and Vishnu. The consequences of the battle would have been the destruction of the whole world. Brahma was greatly alarmed at the situation and appeased the Goddess Jagdamba, who finally appeared and separated the two fighters. As Jagdamba thus saved the world from destruction, She was called the Mediator of Peace or the Goddess of Peace, Shri Shanta Durga.

About the origin of Shri Mangesh the legend runs as follows:

> Once Brahma being very proud of his creative power did not pay due respect to Maheshwara (Shiva). Knowing Brahma's pride, Maheshwara became indignant and started destroying the whole creation of Brahma. Brahma, finding his creation being lost in the fierce anger of Maheshwara,

> became terribly frightened. He hurriedly came down to Mongir or Mongirish Hill near Trihottrapur in the East (Bengal-Mithila region) and stooped down to appease the angry God. Pleased by Brahma's invocation, Maheshwara stopped the destruction. Brahma installed a *linga* at Mongir Hill which was dedicated by the name of Mangesh.

Another version of the legend about Shri Mangesh is as follows:

> Once Parvati, wife of Shiva, got annoyed with her husband over a game of chess and left her abode in Mount Kailash. Wandering away in the jungle She was attacked by a tiger. And frightened as She was at the sight of the beast She invoked Her husband, shouting in terrible affliction: *Mama Gaurisha trahi* (Rescue me O Gaurisha). This tiger was none other than Shiva himself in disguise. Shiva appeared in his real form and the tiger vanished. The expression *mama Gaurisha* later gave rise to Mangarish or Mangesh, the names by which Shiva is invoked.

Interestingly it is the Mangesh who takes the place of *Kuladeva* of the Brahmans of Trihottrapur belonging to Vatsa and Kaundilya *gotras*.

THE UPHEAVAL

So long as the Maurya, Chalukya and other Hindu dynasties ruled Goa, the Gaud-Saraswats and their descendants found adequate protection. But the trouble arose by the beginning of the 14th century and increased gradually. The Muslims invaded Goa about A.D. 1313 and demolished all Hindu temples which came to their notice. They carried away gold and jewellery from the temples, broke up the images and killed priests who dared to resist them. The whole of Goa was ruined. After the Muslims, the Portuguese set foot on Goa. They proved to be no less intolerant and vandalic than their predecessors, and harassed the people in the most inhuman way. On the top of it, they wanted to force their religion upon the Hindus or else they were to lose their land and life or both. The storm of conversion which rose to a peak by A.D. 1541 swept away all the important Hindu shrines and temples; and the deities and their devotees went underground. It was during this upheaval that the images of Shri Shanta Durga and Shri Mangesh were brought from their original places to Ponda, which was then in the hands of Sundherkar, a Hindu Karnatak king belonging to the Lingayat sect. With these deities came those Gaud-Saraswats who were more scrupulous about their religion and who had escaped Portuguese massacre. This is how Ponda became the seat of Hindu deities and a place of refuge for them, although by A.D. 1763 Ponda too was seized by the Portuguese.

SHRI SHANTA DURGA TEMPLE

The present temple of Shri Shanta Durga is situated in the picturesque village of Queula, 3 km off the main road from Ponda. Following the incursion of the Portuguese the deity was brought here from Quelossim in 1564. For three years or so the devotees found no suitable place to build a temple for the deity as no good omen was visible. At last, one night the deity appeared in a dream before the chief priest and expressed her desire to be installed at a place which was then occupied by the Mahars, an untouchable caste. On the following morning when the head priest reported his dream to the Mahajans of Shri Shanta Durga, the ardent devotees approached the Mahars to vacate the land for the temple at any price that the Mahars might demand. But no amount of persuasion or temptation could move the Mahars. Finally, the Mahars said that they would agree to vacate the land for Shri Shanta Durga on condition that they would be granted the right of entrance into the temple once every year. There was no other choice before the Mahajans since the deity wanted to be installed there. Ultimately they had to yield to this demand. Every year on the 6th day of *Magh Shukla* (January), the Mahars enter the temple with their musical instruments and sing songs in honour of the deity. They return home with *prasad* (rice, coconut, flowers and some cash) and a piece of cloth worn by the deity, which are given to them as a mark of honour by the head priest. Soon after the Mahars leave the place, the temple is cleaned and the deity is purified with the holy water of the Ganga.

The temple of Shri Shanta Durga is comparatively massive in structure and elegant in outline. The betel-nut and coconut garden around the temple adds beauty to the natural setting. The temple has a sacred *tolli*, a majestic *khamba* in front, and huge *agarshalas* on either side. In the ground-plane of the temple, besides the *chouko* and the *garbhakud* there is a hall and the side-galleries where non-Hindus can also be accommodated. The image of the temple shows Shri Shanta Durga in the middle and Shiva and Vishnu on either side.

Temple servants

Like most of the temples of Goa, the temple of Shri Shanta Durga too has a number of servants who are paid by the management and whose duty is to serve the deity faithfully according to the nature of the job they are entrusted with. The organization of the temple servants of Shri Shanta Durga has been shown in Table 9.1.

TABLE 9.1 : **Showing the organization of Shri Shanta Durga**

Designation of temple servant	No. of persons	Function
1	2	3
Abhisheki	2	To adorn the deity with *kum-kum*, flowers garlands, etc.
Pujari	4	To bathe, to dress and to worship the deity.
Jotkar	1	To make lighting arrangements inside the temple.
Puranik	1	To recite tales from the *Puranas* and holy books in honour of the deity.
Haridas	1	To sing *kirtan* and *bhajan* in honour of the deity.
Vetradhar or Katkar	1	Shaft-bearer and door-keeper.
Vajantri	17	To play on musical instruments.
Chaughadewala	6	To beat a special kind of drum called *chaughada*.
Masalchi	2	To bear torches during the procession.

TABLE 9.1—*contd.*

1	2	3
Sipahi	4	To guard the temple.
Kalawantani or Devadasis	10 (families)	The dancing girls whose job is to dance and to sing in honour of the deity.
Mridangi	1	To play on a particular kind of drum called *mridang*.
Taldharnare	1	A musician who gives *tal* on a musical instrument called *tabla*.
Bhawin	2	She is either a spinster or a widow who devotes her whole time in *bhajan-kirtan* with a special kind of musical instrument called *tambora*.
Dewe lawanare	2	To make lighting arrangements outside the main temple.
Jhad lot darnare	4	Sweepers.
Sonar	1	Goldsmith.
Sutar	1	Carpenter.
Lohar	1	Ironsmith.
Tanwat	1	Coppersmith.

Besides these servants of the deity, there is a head priest called Bhatji who is in charge of the temple services. He is revered for his direct communion with the deity. He reads the omen from the flowers that drop round the image and communicates the prayers of the devotee to the deity. He belongs to the lineage of the Gaud-Saraswats; but while other Gaud-Saraswats take fish and flesh, he lives on a strictly vegetarian diet. He is expected to live with utmost purity like a *sannyasi*, although he is allowed to lead a married life.

Temple festivals

In addition to the daily routine of worship which is followed by invocation through music and dance, there are periodical functions on the 5th day of every fortnight when the deity is taken out in a procession for a palanquin-ride inside the temple premises. Special functions are arranged on *Vaisakha Shukla Panchami*, *Navaratra*, *Dasahara*, *Kojagari* and also on the day of *Banbhojan* around the end of the month of *Kartika*. The annual function (popularly called *Yatra*), which is the greatest function of the temple, begins on *Magha Shukla Pratipada* (1st day of *Magha Shukla*) and lasts for about six days. During this function, the Mahajans of Shri Shanta Durga make it a point to have a glimpse of the deity, at least, once; and for this they come from distant places with their wives and children and join the community feast arranged by them on the 4th day. The biggest congregation is seen on the 5th night when the deity is taken on palanquin-ride and chariot-drive. The ceremony is kept on for the whole night and till then nobody should retire. On the 6th day, the Mahars enter the temple according to the old custom, and the function comes to an end.

During all these functions the rituals are performed according to the Brahmanical method. Something may be said here about the vehicle of the deity—her palanquin-ride and chariot-drive. On the occasions when the deity goes for a planquin-ride, a large procession follows her devotedly. The priests, the musicians, the dancing girls, and other temple servants, the Mahajans and the peasant folk follow one another in the procession. The deity is carried on their shoulders in a silver palanquin. The procession starts after the Devadasis have sung a prayer in honour of the deity. During the ride there are several halts called *pene* where the procession rests a while, the *Devadasis* sing and dance, and again the ride is resumed. On the night of the annual fair, the deity has a chariot-drive too. A huge four-wheeled wooden chariot, about 40 feet high, is pulled by the Mahajans, the temple servants and others who want to be blessed. The head priest and the Swami of Queula monastery, the latter actually inaugurating this chariot-ride, occupy their places on the chariot along with the deity.

As the proper image of the deity cannot be removed from her seat, four golden replicas have been made for outings. Thus while one replica of the image is carried in a palanquin, the other remains in the chariot, and the third sits on a *jharokha* to attend the dance drama programme.

There are two significant points about the movement of the deity: (1) The deity moves in the palanquin or the chariot only during the night and, therefore, all the functions must be over before the day breaks. (2) The deity rides on two different vehicles at a time. Elsewhere in India, the palanquin and the chariot are used separately on separate occasions; and besides that, the chariot drive is only during the day.

Management of the temple

The temple is managed by an administrative board whose members are chosen from the families of the Mahajans. A Secretary, a Treasurer, and a Mokhtiar are elected once in three years and the President is appointed by the government. The annual income of the temple is nearly 20,000 rupees which comes from gifts and agricultural produce from lands vested in the temple. The temple owns landed property, gold and silver worth several thousands of rupees.

QUEULA MONASTERY

Not far from the temple of Shri Shanta Durga is the famous Queula monastery whose Swami is associated with the chariot-ride of Shri Shanta Durga.

The Gaud-Saraswats of Goa are divided into two sects: the Smartas or Shaivites and the Vaishnavites. The prelate of the Shaivites, called Swami, has his chief monastery in Queula adjacent to the temple of Shri Shanta Durga. The Swami has to make the vow of celibacy and he forsakes all worldly pleasure. He chooses a young disciple who is to succeed him in prelacy. When he dies his corpse is not cremated but is buried instead, and a *samadhi* is raised on the grave in his honour. He uses the title of Gaudpadacharya and receives the highest honour amongst the people of his sect. During all the functions in the temple of Shri Shanta Durga he is invited and it is he who inaugurates the ceremony of chariot-ride.

The Vaishnavites have two main monasteries: one at Gokarna and the other at Partagale, both within the administrative area of Canacona. The prelate of the Queula monastery uses the title of Saraswati at the end of his name, while that of Partagale calls himself Tirtha.

OBSERVATIONS

Almost all the temples of Goa are organized in the pattern observed at Shri Shanta Durga. These temples, as a matter of fact, are not only the places where rituals can be performed and religious fervour satisfied; but, by and large, they have other functions also. It is through these temples that the Gaud-Saraswats of Goa experience the real warmth of the lineage relationship. Usually, in a large society where caste system exists, the clan or the lineage members do not feel among themselves the actual bond of kinship; firstly because no direct genealogical relationship can be traced out; and, secondly, in the absence of any material evidence, there remains only a legendary kinship. In Goa, the Mahajans of a temple who form a lineage group, have a temple in common to refer to, a deity in common to worship, a common ritual to perform, and once in a year a community feast to dine together. These behaviours are the manifestations of kinship bondage, and through them all the temple remains a great symbol. It has been observed that sometimes these temples regulate marriage. The Mahajans of Shri Shanta Durga prefer to have marriage alliances with the Mahajans of Shri Mangesh. Thus the temple symbolizes the lineage, vitalizes the kinship bonds and unites its members to live under a common roof.

We have seen earlier, that the temples of Goa employ a large number of musicians and dancing girls. The musicians have a special role in the temple activities. In course of time these temples have proved to be helpful in producing great performers of instrumental as well as vocal music. Today, one of the most celebrated singers of the country, Lata Mangeshkar, comes from the temple of Shri Mangesh. But unfortunately the system is gradually dying out.

Lastly, a few words may be said about the towering faith of the Gaud-Saraswats. Reference has already been made to the Portuguese method of forcible conversion which disturbed the whole social life of the Goanese. It disrupted the family, separated sons from parents, brothers from brothers, and sisters from sisters. All this happened under cruel circumstances. One accepted Christianity not because he believed in the gospel of Christ, but because he loved life more than religion. The inevitable result of this method of conversion was that the Portuguese could not strike the hard core of Hindu religion which was deeply rooted in the heart of the converts. There are Brahman Christians and Maratha Christians in the villages of Goa who maintain *tulasi-vrindavana* in their houses and who stiil perform some Hindu folk rituals during birth, marriage, illness and such other occasions. Their women might wear western dress and sport the bobbed style of hair; but many of them have not removed the bangles from their hands. Converted Gaud-Saraswats continue to maintain some relationship with their lineage deity. At the time of marriage, they offer coconut, rice and betel-leaves to the deity. During the harvest of new crops, one *seer* (little less than 1 kg) of grain is kept for the deity. This system is called *pad*. On the night of the *yatra* too, many converts attend the functions of their lineage deity. There are many other things which give sufficient evidence of the light maintained by Hindu faith in the hearts of the Christians of Goa. And this is due to the temples which stand as a symbol of faith and solidarity.

10

THE LADAKHI RITUAL OF CREMATION

ENCLOSED by the Western Himalayas and the Karakoram mountains there lies the most fascinating district of Ladakh. Situated on the eastern part of the Kashmir Valley, across the Zoji-la, it is annexed to Jammu & Kashmir for administrative purposes. Linguistically as well as culturally it has a closer affinity with Lahul and Spiti in Himachal Pradesh. The evidence on record shows that it has been a part of India from time immemorial. The Ladakhis themselves hold the view that Buddhism penetrated into Ladakh and even spread beyond the Indus to Tibet and China by the missionary zeal of the Kashmiri monks who went to these levels in or around B.C. 243.

The population of Ladakh is predominantly Buddhist. There are a few Moslems and very few Christians of the Moravian Church. The Christians are now disappearing from Ladakh, but the Moslems are increasing through proselytization.

Culturally, the Ladakhis may be broadly classified into four groups: Dogpa, Balti, Changpa and Ladakhi. The Baltis of Baltistan are largely Moslems, but the Changpa nomads of eastern Ladakh are exclusively Buddhists. There are both Buddhists and Moslems among the Dogpas of Kargil and Skardu. The Buddhists of Ladakh proper consider both the Dogpa and the Changpa as inferior.

The social dichotomy of the Ladakhi Buddhists rests on

sacerdotal and secular considerations. The Lamas (the Superior ones) form a sacerdotal organization with the *sKushok* as its head. The spirit of the *sKushok* is that of some Bodhisattvas. He is born, not made. After his death he is reborn only as *sKushok*. Next to him are *Gelong*, *Gesjyan* and *Gechhul* in order of superiority. The nuns are the *Chomos*. In the secular organization or the organization of the *Jikh-tenpa*, the *rGyalpo* (king) and the *Lonpo* (ministers) are at the apex, although kingship has now been abolished. The *Lharje* (physicians) and the *Onpo* (astrologers) are inferior to them, but held superior to the *Mangriks* (commoners) who constitute peasants, shepherds, and artisans. At the lowest level of the society are the untouchables called *rKsngan*. All the four classes are endogamous and are further subdivided on the basis of occupation. They are polyandrous by tradition, but have now in most cases adopted monogamy by law.

Ladakhi Buddhism is identical with Lamaism. It comes under the Mahayana School of Buddhist discipline which lays emphasis on *bhakti* (fervent devotion) and *puja* (worship) of the Hindu kind. There are innumerable Hindu gods and goddesses which the Ladakhis worship under different names. The elements of ancient Hinduism or early Buddhism are conspicuous in the various aspects of Ladakhi culture. The present note on the ritual of cremation is based on the data collected in 1964.

The Ladakhi term for death is *shiva*. As soon as somebody dies in the family the lamas and the *phasphuns* (members of the sub-lineage) are called. The lama mutters a *mantra* (prayer) and lightens an earthen lamp. He thereafter pulls up the *hair* of the dead so that the life-force (soul?) may come out easily. It is believed that there are two *ushnins* (holes) in the skull. One is *uma*, another is *skyanma*. It is through these holes that the *samjeet* (life-force) comes out at the time of death. The next stage is the bathing of the dead and tying up the corpse in a squatting posture. It is followed by wrapping it in a white shroud called *roras*. The dead is bathed by family members and wrapped in a shroud by the *phasphuns* or members of the sub-lineage. The corpse is kept in the *chhot-khang* (prayer room of the house) and covered by another piece of cloth. It is left there in this condition until the auspicious day for cremation arrives. Usually after five, seven or nine days such a propitious day comes according to astrological calculation. If no auspicious day falls within a fortnight or so, the family plough, yoke, and harrow are kept on the roof of the house where the dead body is placed, and then the cremation follows. During all these days of waiting the lamas come with their ritual instruments to perform a fire-sacrifice called *chingshek* or *jingshek*. The *phasphuns* are very important on this occasion. They feed the bereaved family, sleep in the prayer room and guard the corpse until it is cremated.

On the appointed day the *phasphuns* bring the corpse to the exit and load it on the back of the executioner on whom the main work of cremation rests. The corpse is then laid on a *remes* (bier) and carried to the cremation ground. Every *phasphun* has his *turthot* (funeral oven), usually a little off the village. Only men participate in the funeral procession, while the women are left in the house to weep and mourn. The lamas lead the procession while the *phasphuns* and others follow. When they reach the cremation ground the bier is laid down and all the relatives circumambulate three times clockwise and bow their heads without any consideration of age, sex, and degree of kinship. The family members, excepting the chief mourner, return home soon after performing this rite. The corpse is laid in the funeral oven, whereupon the lamas perform a fire-sacrifice with rice, millet, barley, pea, sesamum, flowers, jaggery, *umbu* and many other herbs, roots of various kinds of grasses, and wood. When it is half-burnt, a piece of bone is taken out by the lama and kept in a *khataks* (scarf). The relic is called *thhus*. When this is over, the *phasphuns* add more fuel to the oven so that the corpse may be completely burnt. After performing the funeral the lamas return to the deceased's house while playing on ritual trumpets.

The bone brought by the lamas is kept in the *chhot-khang* which in the meanwhile has been kept clean by the female *phasphuns*. The lamas are sumptuously fed and given almost all the personal belongings of the deceased, namely clothes, ornaments and utensils. One-fourth of this gift is given to the *gompa* (monastery), to which they belong, and the rest is either sold or used by the lamas themselves. All the members who were in the funeral procession are given sweetmeats to eat, *chhang* (malt beer) to drink and also paid some money which is equally distributed among them. This ceremony is called *srang-chhang*.

FIG. 2 : *The Ladakhi funeral oven* (*turthot*)

On the fourth day, the *phasphuns* and a member of the family of the deceased go to the cremation ground at the end of the midnight to collect relics. The lamas also reach there in time. The skull is kept for making a *stupa*, but the ashes and the bones are thrown into a running stream, after they have been duly sanctified by the lamas. It is on this day that the lamas forecast the new birth of the deceased by looking into some mysterious symbols in the ashes. The skull is powdered and mixed with clay, parched grains, herbs and perfumes. The entire substance is then kneaded and a *stupa* is made thereof. The *stupa* is called *chachha* which the lamas worship for the whole day. After one month it is worshipped again. On the 49th day it is finally immersed after the performance of an elaborate ceremony presided over by the lamas.

The corpses of children below eight years are not bound with string, as in the case of grown-up persons. They are buried on the cliff of the mountain where wild animals may not dig them up. No music is played on this occasion, excepting the small prayer bell *tilbu*. Persons dying of cholera, small-pox, or other epidemic diseases are also buried without musical performance. People believe that disease spreads when music is played on. Persons committing suicide or women who have died in pregnancy are cremated. But those who die of typhoid or high fever are first buried for about a month or two, and later on cremated in the funeral oven.

Those who have been declared as "great souls" by astrologers are not cremated in the common funeral oven of their *phasphun*. Such persons, called *skewa thanbo*, are cremated in the kitchen garden of their house. The cremation ground of the lamas is separate from the *Jikhtenpa*. The *sKushok* is cremated in the *gompa* premises. The *rGyalpo* and the *Lonpo* have also separate cremation grounds and also a different type of funeral oven. The *turthot* of the common people is a simple four-walled structure, about 3 feet in height and almost of the same length and width. It has a perforated platform over which the corpse is placed in the squatting posture from the top, and burnt through a stoke hole provided on one side. It resembles a pottery kiln. In the *turthot* made for the lamas, the *rGyalpo* and the *Lonpo* there is a roof on the top of it, and the corpse is loaded from the side, the opening of which is temporarily sealed at the time of burning.

The Changpa nomads have different customs for the disposal of the dead. They generally mutilate the body into pieces and expose it to wild birds and beasts. The practice is believed to be endowed with religious merit for the deceased. There is a story of one Bodhisattva who once met a starving tigress which was unable to give milk to her cubs. He offered himself as her prey, and thereby saved the life of the beast and her progeny. The Changpas also sometimes tie a boulder round the neck of the corpse and throw it into the river. These practices are common only in the high plateau such as Chumantang, Chushul, Changchenmo, and the areas bordering Tibet where wood is scarce.

The Dogpas follow almost the entire Hindu method of cremation. They do not make use of the *turthot*, described about the central Ladakhi. The speciality of their custom is to cremate the dead with its head to the west. In their case, apricot wood is essential for burning. It is believed that if green apricot trees with fruits and flowers are burnt in the funeral pyre, it would bring peace and happiness to the deceased in heaven. Once the body has been burnt, the ashes and the bones are made into the shape of a small *stupa*. After being kept for a year in the house, the stupa is placed in one of the many *chhortens* (dedicatory pyramidal structure) which form the cultural landscape of the Ladakhi villages and are owned by lineage members among the lay people or monasteries for the monks. This custom of placing the relics of the deceased in the holy *chhorten* is widely prevalent in Ladakh, both among the Ladakhi proper and the Dogpas. The data on the Balti Buddhists could not be collected.

The malignant spirit of the dead, called *shinde*, is believed to take the form of a cat, a dog, or such other animals. To ward off its evil influences on the family, the lamas perform a magical rite, called *shod-long*. A parched grain model of a mule mounted by a man is dragged and beaten with a stick for some time, while chanting *mantras*, and then finally thrown off the house. Householders participate in this mimetic magical rite. To give peace to the departed soul, the astrologers recommend the name of a deity to be painted in a silken scroll and hung in the prayer room of the family. The scroll is known as *lha-skul* or the painting of God.

All the relatives who had touched the corpse observe pollution for a month. After the death of a husband, the wife has to observe mourning for a period of one year during which she is not supposed to come out of the courtyard of her house. She does not wear *peyark* (head-gear) and other ornaments. She dresses in a black woollen garment, called *chhali*, sleeps in one corner of the house, completely segregated from the rest of the family members, and is tabooed to have sex relations with her other husbands. On the death of the wife the husband(s) must observe the same restriction of dress, movement and sex relation. He has to keep the flaps on either side of his quilted skull-cap hanging down straight. This mark of mourning is observed by all the male members of the family. They also shave their hair and beard on the purification day, which are till then allowed to grow. The women wash their hair. All the members must bathe in hot water before they give a feast to the lamas.

The death anniversary, *shizak*, is observed at least for three years, when the soul of the dead is worshipped by the lamas. Feast is thrown to the *phasphuns* on each occasion. A little quantity of food is offered on a flat stone by the sister's son. Again on the *losar* (new year's day), the *shinpos* (ancestors) are invoked at the cremation ground by offering balls of *sattu* (parched millet flour) and libation of *chhang*. The rite, called *shir*, is performed by the *phasphuns* and the lamas at about 3 o'clock in the morning. Parched grain and saffron are burnt on this occasion. The sacrificial food is finally consumed by the *rKsngan*.

OBSERVATIONS

The Ladakhis adopt four different methods in disposing of their dead; these are, cremation, mutilation, immersion, and burial. The first is the most common, the last is only under special conditions, while the other two are regional and perhaps due to ecological causes. Most religions like Zoroastrianism, Christianity and Islam have particular customs for disposal of the dead, which in all cases have to be followed by their adherents. Although cremation is common in Brahmanical Hinduism several sects like the Lingayat, Bishnoie, and *sannyasis* regularly bury their dead. The custom of burying a pregnant woman and infant is also in vogue. There is the *Pauranic* reference of Dadhichi who allowed a cow to lick his body to death so that the gods might arm themselves with his bones and gain easy victory over the demons. The Ladakhi's belief of religious merit by exposing the dead to wild animals and the story of Bodhisattva offering himself to the tigress to save the lives of the cubs, find a parallel in the Zoroastrian and Brahmanical Hindu idea of gaining religious merit by offering the body.

As it transpires from the preceding discussion, the Ladakhi Buddhists are highly under the influence of soul-spirit complex. The pulling up of the hair of the deceased, tying up the dead body in a squatting posture, mortuary room, circumambulation of the corpse, the forecast by the lamas of the new birth, the malignant spirit of the dead taking the form of animals, performance of mimetic magical rites to ward off ghosts, ancestor-worship, rules of pollution, annual *pinda* offering and libation to the ancestors and fire sacrifice are some of the most significant customs which are perhaps due to a synthesis of Brahminical Hinduism, Buddhism, and the old Bon religion of the Ladakhis.

One of the most interesting elements in the Ladakhi method of cremation is the funeral oven called *turthot*. Those who have seen the Buddhist *stupa* at Sanchi, Karle and the like would find an amazing similarity between this and the funerary oven (see Fig. 2 p. 150) of the Ladakhis. The present writer does not know of a similar practice anywhere else. The ancient Buddhist *stupas* which are structurally similar to the *turthot*, as we are told by archaeologists, possess the relics of the Buddha and his disciples, and are, therefore, functionally different from the latter. At this point, it may be stated that the Ladakhi Buddhists have a different dedicatory structure called *chhorten* which is a holy receptacle for the relics of the ancestors. The *chhorten* is an inverted and truncated cone, the basement of which is square. It is sometimes pronounced as *chhodten*, and is perhaps derived from the Sanskrit *chaitya*, an offering receptacle. We are unable to give any satisfactory explanation of the evolution of the funeral oven and its functional correlation with the ancient Buddhist *stupas*. Archaeologists may perhaps throw some light on the subject.

Lastly, it may be pointed out that the Ladakhi term *shiva* for death seems to be theologically significant. The Brahmanical classical God of the same name, Shiva, who is identified with Rudra, the God of death.

GLOSSARY

abhiseka (*abhiṣeka*)	A form of worship, sprinkling or dripping water over an idol of god, generally Śiva liṅga.
Advaita	Nondualism; spiritual insight which sees ultimate reality as being neither monistic nor dualistic.
Agnihotra	A Brahman who performs fire-sacrifice daily, morning and evening.
akhara (*akhārā*)	An abode of the Nāgā ascetic; a wrestling ground.
akkhadapan (*akkhaḍapana*)	Headstrong.
anumarana (*anumaraṇa*)	Following one's husband in death, by immolating herself on his funeral pyre; the *sati* practice.
arati (*āratī*)	The waving of a lamp in the ritual of worship; various objects, including a lighted lamp, are waved before the deity, accompanied by *mantra*, etc.
artha	"Wealth, power, purpose"; one of the four *puruṣarthas*, the pursuit of wealth and power.
ashrama (*āśrama*)	An abode of an ascetic; one of the four stages of Hindu life: student, householder, forestdweller, and renouncer.
ashvamedha (*aśvamedha*)	The Vedic horse-sacrifice; a fertility rite performed at the consecration of a king.

asthi-visarjana	Throwing of the bones, which remain after cremation, into a holy river.
asura	Spiritual, incorporeal, divine; in the RV the highest spirit God (from *asu*, life, spiritual life); Varuṇa is said to be an *asura*; later the meaning changes entirely, *asura* (*a-sura*, "not-God") means a demon or an evil spirit opposed to the *devas*.
atisaya-kshetra (*atisaya-kṣetra*)	The places of Jain pilgrimage which have assumed importance because of temples, idols, or certain miraculous events.
avachya (*avācya*)	Not expressible in words, unutterable, unspeakable; the last word of the Upaniṣada about Brahman.
Avatar (*avatāra*)	The "descent" of a god; an incarnation, especially of Viṣṇu.
avidya (*avidyā*)	Ignorance, absence of the true and liberating knowledge, often identified with *māyā* and cause of illusion and delusion.
Avimukta	The "Never-forsaken", a name of Vārānasi; a place which frees from sin (*avi*).
Balarama (*Balarāma*)	A younger brother of Lord Jagannāth.
bali	Sacrifice.
Banarasi (*banārasi*)	A citizen of Banāras (Vārānasi), distinguished by a style of life and attitude of *masti*, *akkhaḍapana*, and *phakkaḍapana*.
bhanga (*bhaṇga*)	The intoxicating hemp, *cannabis sativa*.
bhoga	Experience of pleasure or pain; enjoyment; an offering to the deity.
bilva	The wood-apple tree, with clusters of three or five leaves used in the worship of Śiva.

bir (*bīr*)	A folk deity, related with the cult of *yaksha*; a deified "hero" (*vīra*).
Brahma (*Brahmā*)	The creator god, having four heads, one to look in each direction.
brahmalina (*brahmalīna*)	Merging with the "Absolute" (Brahman), after death.
buddha-kshetra (*buddha-kṣetra*)	Buddha-field, region or world, or world system in which a particular Buddha lives and operates.
Chalanti-Vishnu (*Chalanti-Viṣṇu*)	The "Mobile Viṣṇu", an epithet of the king of Puri.
Chariyageeti (*Chariyāgīti*)	A Buddhist text, containing *sandhyā* terms.
chaturvarga	The four aims of life: *dharma, artha, kāma* and *mokṣa*.
chhorten (*chhoḍten*)	A dedicatory pyramidal structure (Ladākhi), perhaps derived from the Sanskrit *caitya*.
Dalai Lama (*Dalāi Lāmā*)	The spiritual head of Tibetan Buddhism.
dana (*dāna*)	Gift, alms giving; one of the religious duties of the householder.
danda (*daṇda*)	The sacred staff carried by some ascetics, especially the Daṇdī (the one who carries *daṇda*), a section of the Dasnāmi sannyasi order.
danda pranama (*daṇda praṇāma*)	Measuring of the length of the pilgrim's body by successive prostrations on the ground.
Dandi (*Daṇḍi*)	An ascetic belonging to one of the sections of the Dasnāmi sannyasi order.
darshana (*darśana*)	The "auspicious sight" of the deity or a saint.
dhama (*dhāma*)	The abode of God; one of the four principal sacred places of Hindu pilgrimages: Puri, Rāmeshwaram, Dwārkā, and Badrināth.
dharma	Meritorious duty, religious duty, religious law; one of the four

	puruṣārthas, the pursuit of righteousness; that which holds the world together; in modern usage religious tradition.
dharna (*dharnā*)	A rite of fasting and lying for three days and three nights in a temple, to seek the God's grace.
dikapala (*dikapāla*)	A deity posted at the entrance of the temple to guard from evil spirits.
Gajendra-moksha (*Gajendra-mokṣa*)	A *Paurānic* episode of God Viṣṇu protecting an elephant from the clutches of a crocodile.
gana (*gaṇa*)	A deity posted at the entrance of the temple to guard from evil spirit.
garbha-griha (*garbha-gṛha*)	The sanctum sanctorum.
garbha-vasa (*garbha-vāsa*)	Living in a *tīrtha* for nine months, not crossing its sacred territory.
ghatia (*ghātiā*)	A Brahman priest who has jurisdiction over a small section of the ghat where he tends to the needs of the pilgrims; also called Gangā-putra, the "son of the (river) Gangā".
godana (*godāna*)	A ritual of gifting a cow.
gompa (*gompā*)	A Buddhist monastery (Ladākhi).
guna (*guṇa*)	Strands of *prakṛiti* (nature): *sattva* (goodness), *rajas* (energy), and *tamas* (dullness); quality, property.
guru-bhai (*guru-bhāī*)	The disciple of the same teacher and mentor.
Jagannath (*Jagannāth*)	The "Lord of the universe", the name of Viṣṇu-Kṛṣṇa at the temple of Puri in Orissa.
Jamboo dwipa (*Jambu dwīpa*)	The *Paurānic* territory within which lies the country of Bhārata (that is India).
Janmastami (*Janmāṣtami*)	The festival celebrating the birth of Lord Kṛṣṇa.

Jhoolana (*Jhulana*)	A festival of swinging God, especially Kṛṣṇa and Rāma.
jivanamukta (*jīvanamukta*)	"Liberated while alive"; the highest category of saint or realised person who has reached the goal in this life in the human body.
Jyotirlinga (*jyotirliṅga*)	"The Liṅga of Light", a manifestation of Śiva as a luminous column, traditionally located at twelve holy places in India.
kaivalya	Isolation, solitude, detachment; a spiritual state of supreme freedom.
kala tirtha (*kāla tīrtha*)	*Tīrtha* in the form of auspicious time.
kalivarjya	Prohibited practice in *kali yuga.*
kalpa-vasa (*kalpa-vāsa*)	Living religiously in a *tīrtha* for one month.
kama (*kāma*)	The creative power of desire, personified as God of love; one of the four *puruṣarthas*, the pursuit of passion, pleasure.
karma	The totality of human action, including the burden of deeds from previous existence.
karmakandi (*karmakāndi*)	The priest competent for performing Vedic sacrifices.
karpatika (*karpatikā*)	The pilgrim's apparel, namely a copper ring, a copper-bracelet, and a red robe.
Kashi-vasa (*Kāśī vāsa*)	Living in Kāśi with religious motive.
Kavya Purusha (*Kāvya Puruṣa*)	The Spirit of Poetry.
kshetra-pal (*kṣetra-pāla*)	A deity protecting fields; an epithet of Śiva.
kshetra-sannyasa (*kṣetra-saṁnyāsa*)	A vow to dwell within the sacred territory of a *tīrtha* till death.
kshetrastha (*kṣetrastha*)	Residing at a sacred place.
Kumbha	A jar, vessel; a symbol of fullness; a festive occasion when the conjunction of the planet Jupiter takes place

	with Aquarius, or with Aries, Sun and Capricorn, or with Leo, held once in twelve years at Hardwāra, Prayāga, Ujjain and Nāsik.
kunda (*kuṇd*)	A sacred pool for bathing.
kusothar	The ritual of sitting on a *kusa*-grass-mat in a temple precinct, observing abstinence (taking only fruits and milk) and praying the deity for the desired object until the deity responds favourably.
lama (*lāmā*)	The superior one (Ladākhi), a Mahāyāna ascetic.
lila (*līlā*)	Divine play, the world viewed as God's sport; a *Paurānic* concept, not Vedic.
linga (*liṅga*)	A phallic symbol representing Śiva, normally carved from stone.
lokeshana (*lokeṣaṇā*)	The desire for worldly gains.
madhukari (*madhukari*)	Taking food from five or more houses (collected in alms), like honeybees.
Mahakala (*Mahākāla*)	The great destroyer, an epithet of Śiva.
mahapataka (*mahāpātaka*)	Guilty of Brāhmaṇ murder, drinking of *sura*, theft of Brāhmaṇ's gold, and incest.
mahaprasada (*mahāprasāda*)	The flesh of the sacrificial animal; the rice offered to the Lord of Jagannatha Puri.
mahashāshana (*mahasmāśāna*)	The great cremation ground; a name of Vārānasi.
mahatmya (*mahātmya*)	The glorification of a deity or a sacred place.
mahatmya grantha (*mahātmya grantha*)	Eulogistic literature.
mandala (*maṇḍala*)	The "circle" or circular diagram of the sacred universe in symbolic paintings; a sacred zone, larger than *kṣetra*.

manokamanalinga (*manokāmanāliṅga*)	The *liṅga* whose worship is efficacious in fulfilling all desires; an epithet of Lord Baidyanatha, a form of Śiva.
mantra	A sacred mythical formula, holy word or verse; being a powerful word it can also have the meaning of spell or incantation.
masti (*mastī*)	Ardent passion, wantonness, *joi de vivre*.
maya (*māyā*)	The cosmic illusion, the illusory quality of this transitory world; the false perception of the world as permanent, a synonym for ignorance.
moksha (*mokṣa*)	Liberation of soul, absolute freedom; the state of release from the bondage of the chain of birth, death and rebirth.
mokshadayini (*mokṣadāyinī*)	The bestower of *mokṣa*.
mukti-kshetra (*mukti-kṣetra*)	A sacred place of salvation.
neti-neti	"Not this, not this" (*na iti*), the denial of any characterization of the Atman or Brahma in the Upaniṣad; pure apophatism.
nirvana (*nirvāṇa*)	"The blowing out (of the flame)" final extinction, consumption of all thinkable limitations, including time, space and being; liberation, the ultimate goal (mainly in Jainism and Buddhism).
Panda (*Paṇḍā*)	A pilgrim guide, a generic term for many varieties of ritual officiants.
Parvati (*Pārvati*)	"Daughter of the mountain", the wife of Śiva.
Phakkadapan (*phakkaḍapana*)	A Boehmian style of life and state of mind, contended with the bare

	minimum, carefree and unconventional in many respects.
pitar (*pitarah, pitṛ*)	Father, the fore-fathers, ancestors, for whose well-being a son performs the rites of *śraddha* and *tarpana* after death.
pitri-tirtha (*pitṛ-tīrtha*)	A *tirtha* meritorious for performing *śraddha* ritual.
pradakshina (*pradakṣiṇā*)	Going round the idol of the deity clockwise.
pralaya	The cosmic dissolution of the world occurring periodically, after one of the vast aeons of time called *kalpa* or a day of Brahma.
prasada (*prasāda*)	The consecrated food, having been, offered before a deity or a saint; gift, divine grace.
prayaschita (*prāyascita*)	Penance and ritual purification.
punya (*puṇya*)	Religious merit, reward of acts of worship, virtue (its opposite, *papa*).
Purana (*Purāṇa*)	One of the collections of ancient sacred history which traditionally contains authentic account of the ancient days.
Purusa (*Puruṣa*)	The Person, spirit, Man; the primordial Man; the inner Man; the spiritual person in Man; the spiritual principle of reality (its opposite *Prakṛti*).
purushartha (*puruṣārtha*)	The aim of human life, traditionally four: *dharma*, *artha*, *kāma* and *mokṣa*, but the ultimate aim is *mokṣa*.
putreshana (*putreṣana*)	The desire for son.
Radha (*Rādhā*)	The beloved consort of Lord Kṛṣṇa.
Ramanavami (*Rāmanavami*)	The festival celebrating the birth of Lord Rama.
Rasa-lila (*Rāsa-līlā*)	A dance-drama depicting the love of Gopīs (cowherd girls) for Lord

	Kṛṣṇa, commemorating the *Rasa* dance which Kṛṣṇa had lovingly performed in Vṛndavana groves with Gopīs, manifesting himself between each pair of the beautiful maidens.
Ratha-yatra (*Ratha-yātrā*)	A festival in which the deity of a temple make a journey of the chariot; the yearly festival of Lord Jagannatha's procession in Puri; also celebrated in Kaśī.
Rimpoche (*Rimpoce*)	A jewel-like person; an incarnate form of some Bodhisattva (Mahayana Buddhism).
Rishi (*Ṛṣi*)	A seer, sage, wise man; the poet sages to whom the Veda was revealed; a special class of being superior to man and inferior to gods.
Rudra	A Vedic God of storm, later identified with Śiva.
sadhana (*sādhanā*)	Spiritual disciplining of life.
sahagamana	Following one's husband in death, by immolating herself on his funeral pyre; the sati practice.
samadhi (*samādhi*)	A state of deep concentration or absorption; the last of the yogic spiritual stages; the tomb of a holy person.
sampradaya (*saṁpradāya*)	A teaching tradition, begun by the founder of a philosophical school, generally named after that founder.
samskara (*saṁskara*)	"Sacrament", a rite marking the different important events in the life of man (*jātakarman*, *upanayana*, *vivāha*, etc.); *karmic* residues, psychic impressions left by previous lives and influencing to some extent a person's individual existence.
sandhyabhasa (*semdhyā bhāṣa*)	Twilight language, a language of light and darkness, partly light,

	partly darkness, some passages can be understood, others cannot; a high order discourse on *dharma* words which have another, a different meaning from literal meaning.
sangam (*sangama*)	The confluence of rivers.
sanskriti (*saṁskṛti*)	Culture.
saptapuri (*śaptapurī*)	Seven sacred cities of Hindu pilgrimage: Ayodhya, Mathura, Hardwara, Kaśī, Kaṅcī, Ujjain, and Dwarka.
Saraswati (*Saraswatī*)	A title of the Dasnami Śaiva ascetics; the goddess of knowledge; a sacred river.
Shakti (*Śakti*)	The female active power of God (usually Śiva), personified as Goddess who assumes the creative function.
shastra (*śāstra*)	Precept, command, instruction, rule, authoritative teaching; a body of authoritative text or any text containing religious injunctions (*Śruti*) or *Smṛti*).
Shiva (*Śiva*)	The Auspicious One; one of the most important gods of Hindu tradition, the destroyer of the universe (also Brahma, Viṣṇu); the great yogi and model of ascetics.
shiva (*śiva*)	Death (Ladakhi); auspicious, gracious, kind, benevolent (Sanskrit).
Shivaratri (*Śivarātri*)	"The night of Śiva", the greatest festival in honour of Śiva on the fourteenth of the waving fortnight of Phalguna.
shamshana (*śmaśāna*)	A cremation ground.
siddha-kshetra siddhakṣetra	The places where the Tirthankara and other holy men have attained *nirvaṇa*.

sKushok	A spiritual head of the Ladakhi Buddhists, believed to be an incarnate being.
soma	The sacrificial plant from which the *soma*-juice is extracted with elaborate rituals; the sap or drink of immortality (*amṛta*, another name for *soma*) used ritually to enter into a higher state of consciousness.
Samrti (*Smṛti*)	The scriptures coming after the *Śruti* such as epics (*itihasa*), law-books (*dharma-śastra*), etc., and having less authority than the *Śruti* itself, on which they are based.
sraddha (*śrāddha*)	A rite of homage to deceased relatives; offering to the ancestor, generally performed by the son of the deceased and repeated on certain occasions.
stupa (*stūpa*)	A dome-shaped Buddhist monument, enshrining the earthly relics of the Buddha.
Sutra (*Sūtra*)	An aphoristic text that usually cannot be understood without a commentary (*bhaṣya*), belongs to the *Smṛti* and is meant for easy memorizing.
Tantra	A religious system, not based on the Veda, containing of secret doctrines and practices which give access to hidden powers, the interrelation of body and spirit, of matter and soul, *bhukti* (enjoyment) and *mukti* (liberation).
tapas	One of the forms of the primordial energy, along with *kama*; heat, energy, spiritual fervour or ardour; austerity, asceticism, penance believed to be creative, like the brooding heat of a mother hen.

tirtha (*tīrtha*)	A place of pilgrimage; pure and holy.
Tirtha (*Tīrtha*)	A title of the Dasnami Śaiva ascetics.
Tirtha-purohita (*Tīrtha-purohita*)	The priest officiating at the rites performed in a *tirtha.*
Tirtharaj (*Tīrtharaja*)	The king of *tirtha*, a name of Prayaga.
tulasi (*tulasī*)	The sacred basil plant, worshipped in the courtyards of homes and temples, also supplies the beads worn by the Vaiṣṇavas.
tulasi-vrindavana (*tulasī-vṛndāvana*)	A sacred structure containing the basil plant.
turiyatita (*tūriyātītā*)	The highest stage of blessedness when the ascetic considers his body a corpse, maintains no distinctions of caste and creed.
ulatabansi (*ultabānsi*)	An unintelligible variety of mystic poetry, inverting or reversing all common and established meanings, composed by mystics and saints of medieval India (cf. Kabir).
varsavasa (*varṣāvāsa*)	A time of retreat for ascetics and sannyasis, staying at one place during the four months of rainy season (*caturmasa*).
Vishnu (*Viṣṇu*)	"The all penetrating"; one of the three important gods of Hindu tradition, known for the three wide steps with which he measures out the three worlds: the preserver, mainly worshipped in his avatara (cf. Kṛṣṇa, Rama).
Vishwanath (*Viśwanāth*)	"The Lord of the universe", as present in Varanasī.
vitteshana (*vitteṣaṇā*)	The desire for wealth.
Vivaha-panchami (*Vivāha-pañcamī*)	The festival celebrating the wedding of Rāma with Sīta, the daughter of king Janaka.

vrisotsarga (*vṛṣotsarga*)	A death rite of branding the bull on one flank with a discus and on the other flank with a trident, and then letting him loose with four young cows to roam about sportingly.
yajamana (*yajmāna*)	Sacrificer.
Yama	The twin of Yamī, the first man and the first to pass through death and to reach immortality, hence the forerunner for men on the path of death and the ruler in the realm of the dead; Lord of the infernal regions.
Yami (*Yamī*)	The sister of Yama with whom she forms the first pair of humans on earth (According to some texts, although she tempts her brother to commit incest with her, he does not yield to her temptation).
yuga	Generation, one of the four cosmic ages that are repeated in the same order: Kṛta or Satya, Treta, Dvapara, and Kali (the present degenerated age).

INDEX